The Strategy of
Social Protest

The Dorsey Series in Sociology

Editor   ROBIN M. WILLIAMS, JR.
           Cornell University

The Strategy of
Social Protest

WILLIAM A. GAMSON
The University of Michigan

1975 *DP* **The Dorsey Press** Homewood, Illinois 60430

Irwin-Dorsey International London, England WC2H 9NJ
Irwin-Dorsey Limited Georgetown, Ontario L7G 4B3

ISBN 0-256-01684-4
Library of Congress Catalog Card No. 74–12926
Printed in the United States of America

To Mimi

Preface

This book examines the experiences of a representative collection of American voluntary groups that, between 1800 and 1945, have challenged some aspect of the status quo. It explores the strategies they used and the organizational characteristics that influenced the success of their challenges. The results raise some serious questions about the pluralist interpretation of the operation of power in American society.

I suppose it is relatively common to experience, even when engaged in research that one enjoys doing and finds enlightening, a certain frustration. In any effort in which I've been involved, I have found myself preoccupied at certain stages with the limitations of what I am doing. These feelings are troubling when they occur but I have learned to value them. From the seeds of this dissatisfaction, a future research effort may grow.

Thus it was with the work described in this book. By the summer of 1966, I found myself moving toward completion of a study of the Cold War that Andre Modigliani and I had been working on since 1962. Any sense of optimism about the impact of peace research had been snuffed out by the brutal American presence in Vietnam and the surrounding rhetoric which justified this military adventure. Understanding the dynamics of the Cold War conflict still seemed important to me, but I had no illusions that those who waged and justified war in Vietnam would be receptive to any insights or arguments that we might develop.

Another question seemed prior and paramount — what are the levers of change in American society? Two friends of mine at Michigan, Marc Pilisuk and Tom Hayden, had published a stimulating essay addressing many of the issues on my mind. "Is There a Military Industrial Complex Which Prevents Peace?" they asked (Pilisuk and Hayden, 1965). Although I was not completely satisfied by their answer, I was fully persuaded of the value of the quest. Understanding the operation of power in American society seemed necessary for the agenda of peace research.

During the academic year, 1966–67, I began meeting in an informal weekly seminar with two graduate students at Michigan, Samuel Friedman and James McEvoy, to discuss issues of power in American society and how one might fruitfully do research on them. By the end of that year, through some process of alchemy, we found ourselves digging through back issues of the *Missouri Farmer* for 1919 — apparently a far cry from the military-industrial complex. Actually, in our minds it was not a very far cry because we had come to see the permeability of the American political system as the primary issue that we wished to explore and a study of the careers of relatively powerless groups that attempt to make changes as a focus of investigation. The exigencies of doing research have moved us a few steps further from our starting point but I believe that this book still speaks to the original, motivating questions.

Eventually, the ideas we discussed led to a research proposal and the National Science Foundation supported the work with two essential research grants which enabled us to complete it. A large number of people participated at different stages and I find it more natural to use the word "we" in describing this work — not the editorial "we" but a literal one. John Evans joined the project and contributed an important effort in defining the unit of analysis as well as in doing a number of pilot studies on challenging groups. Arnold Lewis made a major contribution to the definition of the outcome of a challenge and helped to design the questionnaire.

Robin Lepore Thomas played a crucial role at two stages. First, as an Antioch co-op student, she and fellow Antiochian Locke Holmes, did the major work on compiling the sampling frame. Later, after graduating, she returned to work full time on the study as supervisor of compiling the protocols on the groups in the sample and of the coding operation. It was largely due to her skillful and energetic efforts that we were able to get both high quality data and reasonable comparability on protocols for 53 groups compiled by 17 different people!

Most of the actual compiling of protocols was done by undergraduates — either Antiochians on co-op jobs or Michigan students. They included Jane Palmer, Mary Lawson, Carl Greenberg, Peter Hunt, Alden Mudge, Steve Gortmaker, Meredith Reid, Grant McCracken, Rick Bent, Paul Karsten, and John Alberti. Nancy Foster came on the project near the end to work full time and did an excellent job on the eight protocols she compiled. Rick Bent also made major contributions to the coding operation.

A number of graduate students also participated during various stages. Dee Wernette made major contributions both in adding to the theoretical clarity of the work and in developing the complicated codes for the outcome of challenges. John Angle, Stanley Presser, and Patricia Pastor worked for shorter periods as part of their NIMH traineeships. Steve Rytina helped in the data analysis phase and Bruce Taylor with the tedious but important job of checking references.

Several people read over an earlier draft of the manuscript and made helpful suggestions: Dee Wernette, Stan Presser, Robin Williams, Zelda Gamson, Stan Kaplowitz, Rudolf Vleeming. My colleague, Chuck Tilly, and his associates have used a draft of this book in a seminar on mobilization for collective action and I have found their ideas and their own work immensely helpful at a number of points. I have been fortunate at both the Center for Research on Conflict Resolution where the project was originally located, and more recently at the Center for Research on Social Organization, in having colleagues whose work was closely related and who offered the kind of intellectual support and stimulation that is so helpful in a project of this sort.

In the end, of course, many of the answers we sought eluded us and I have begun new work in an attempt to remedy the shortcomings of this effort. That is a story for a future preface.

December 1974   WILLIAM A. GAMSON

Contents

chapter one

The Permeability of the Political Arena

In May, 1937, shortly before Memorial Day, 78,000 steelworkers began a strike against the "Little Steel" companies of Bethlehem Steel, Republic Steel, Inland Steel, and Youngstown Sheet and Tube. The CIO-backed Steel Workers Organizing Committee (SWOC) was less than a year old at the time but had already enjoyed some notable success. A few months earlier, it had signed collective bargaining agreements with the five largest U.S. Steel subsidiaries, and, by early May, SWOC had signed contracts with 110 firms.

The Little Steel companies, however, were prepared to resist. Under the leadership of Tom M. Girdler, president of Republic Steel, they refused to sign an agreement which they felt, in Girdler's words, "was a bad thing for our companies, for our employees; indeed for the United States of America" (Galenson, 1960, p. 96).

The decision to resist was made more ominous by the common practice of large employers of the time to stock arsenals of weapons and tear gas in anticipation of labor disputes. Much of our information comes from the report of the LaFollette Committee of

1

the United States Senate,[1] which investigated the events surrounding the Little Steel strike. The committee report noted, for example, that during the years 1933 to 1937, over a million dollars' worth of tear gas and sickening gas was purchased by employers and law-enforcement agencies but that "all of the largest individual purchasers are corporations and that their totals far surpass those of large law-enforcement purchasers" (quoted in Sweeney, 1956, p. 20). The largest purchaser of gas equipment in the country was none other than the Republic Steel Corporation, which "bought four times as much as the largest law-enforcement purchaser." The Republic Steel arsenal included 552 revolvers, 61 rifles with 1325 rounds of ammunition, and 245 shotguns in addition to gas grenades (Sweeney, p. 33).

The Little Steel strike began on May 26, 1937, and for a few days prior to May 30, picketing and arrests occurred near Republic Steel's mill in south Chicago. On Memorial Day, after a mass meeting at strike headquarters, the strikers decided to march to the plant to establish a mass picket line. A crowd of about 1,000 persons, "headed by two bearers of American Flags, . . . started across the prairie toward the street which fronts on the mill. There was a holiday spirit over the crowd" (Sweeney, p. 33).

Chicago police were there in force and the paraders were commanded to disperse. Within a few minutes, seven strikers were dead, three lay fatally wounded, scores of others were seriously wounded, and 35 policemen were injured. The LaFollette Committee concluded on the basis of testimony from many eye-witnesses and photographs that "the first shots came from the police; that these were unprovoked, except perhaps by a tree branch thrown by the strikers, and that the second volley of police shots was simultaneous with the missiles thrown by the strikers." The strikers fled after the first volley but were pursued by the police. Of the ten marchers who were fatally shot, ". . . seven received the fatal wound in the back, three in the side, none in front. . . . The medical testimony of the nature of the marchers' wounds indicates that they were shot in flight. . . . The police were free with their use of clubs as well as guns. . . . Suffice it to say that the evidence, photographic and oral, is replete with instances of the use of clubs upon marchers doing their utmost to retreat, as well as upon those

---

[1] Hearings before a Subcommittee of the Committee on Education and Labor, United States Senate, 75th Congress, (LaFollette Committee). U.S. Government Printing Office, Washington, D.C., 1939.

who were on the ground and in a position to offer no show of resistance," the LaFollette Committee Report concluded (quoted in Galenson, 1960).

The "Memorial Day Massacre" at the Republic Steel Plant in Chicago was the most notorious but by no means the only violent clash in the Little Steel strike. The strike was effectively broken by these tactics. Within two weeks of the Memorial Day clash, the Republic Steel plant had resumed normal operation. Within another few weeks, other struck plants reopened as well and the strike was essentially over.

The victory of the companies was, as it turned out, only a temporary one. By the fall of 1941, all four Little Steel companies had agreed to recognize the SWOC, and in May, 1942, the Steel Workers Organizing Committee became the United Steelworkers of America. Today, the leaders of the union dine with Presidents and serve as labor spokesmen on a variety of governmental bodies. By any measure of membership of the polity, they are full-fledged and certified. In reading the bitter history of the Little Steel strike from the consciousness of today, it is difficult to credit the fact that these events occurred a mere generation ago, in the living memory of many readers or, at the very least, of their parents.

This particular challenger has, for better or worse, moved inside the salon. But the anterooms and corridors contain the battered hulks of less successful challengers. Their abortive careers also promise to tell us important things about the permeability of the American political system.

Take the Brotherhood of the Cooperative Commonwealth, for example. Born in the ferment of the 1890s, it was the brainchild of an obscure Maine reformer, Norman Wallace Lermond. "Its immediate and most important objective was to colonize *en masse* a sparsely inhabited Western state with persons desiring to live in socialist communities. Once established, the colonists would be in a position to capture control of the state's government and lay the foundation for a socialist commonwealth" (Quint, 1964).

Not much happened for the first year of its existence but Lermond was "a letter writing dynamo and he bombarded reformers throughout the country with appeals for assistance." He began to get some results. Imogene C. Fales, a New York reformer, "who was a charter member of innumerable humanitarian and socialist movements in the 1880s and 1890s, agreed to serve with Lermond as co-organizer" (Quint).

But the big catch for the fledgling challenging group was Eugene V. Debs. Debs had been recently released from his prison term for defying the injunction against the American Railway Union which broke the Pullman strike. He was a genuine hero of the left, who was now, for the first time, espousing socialism. Debs was a thoroughly decent person who lacked the vituperative personal style so characteristic of many leftists. Furthermore, he was an extraordinarily effective platform speaker where, as Quint describes him, "the shining sincerity of his speeches and the flowing honesty of his personality more than compensated for the lack of knowledge of the more delicate points of Marxist theory. His soul was filled with a longing for social justice and he communicated this feeling to the audiences who gathered to hear him extol the new Social Democracy."

Debs became attracted to the colonization scheme. "Give me 10,000 men," Debs told a socialist convention, "aye, 10,000 in a western state with access to the sources of production, and we will change the economic conditions, and we will convince the people of that state, win their hearts and their intelligence. We will lay hold upon the reins of government and plant the flag of Socialism upon the State House" (quoted in Quint).

Many other socialists were appalled at what they considered a diversion of energy into a thoroughly impractical scheme. However, they were gentle with Debs personally, hoping to woo him back to the true path. Even the normally vitriolic socialist leader, Daniel DeLeon, was unaccustomedly polite. "With warm esteem for the good intentions of Mr. Debs, but fully appreciative of the harm that more failures will do," he wrote, "we earnestly warn the proletariat of America once more not to embark on this chimera; not to yield out of love for the good intentions of Mr. Debs, greater respect for his judgment than it deserves" (Quint).

Gradually, Debs began relegating the colonization scheme to be one of several strategies rather than to be *the* strategy of the socialist movement. The Brotherhood of the Cooperative Commonwealth did not particularly prosper. They did establish a colony, "Equality" in Edison, Washington, and later another at Burley, Washington, but these did not thrive. "By 1902, Equality contained 105 people, living on a very plain diet in two apartment houses, four log cabins, and fourteen frame houses, earning a bare subsistence by the sale of lumber and grain" (Quint). By 1914, there wasn't anything left of the colonization plans of the Brotherhood of the Cooperative Commonwealth.

How can we account for the different experiences of a representative collection of American challenging groups? What is the characteristic response to groups of different types and what determines this response? What strategies work under what circumstances? What organizational characteristics influence the success of the challenge?

The careers of challenging groups tell us about the permeability and openness of the American political system. To know who gets in and how is to understand the central issue in competing images of the American political experience.

THE PLURALIST IMAGE OF AMERICAN POLITICS

Until the turbulence of the 1960s caused many to rethink the issue, a particular interpretation of American politics dominated the thinking of most professional observers. It remains highly influential today if perhaps not as dominant as it once was in the face of a developing body of criticism. This interpretation presents an image of a highly open system with free access for would-be competitors. Furthermore, the image has behind it a well-developed and elegant body of theoretical ideas usually presented under the label "pluralist democracy" or simply "pluralism."

A democratic political system must be able to handle two great problems if it is to continue successfully: the danger of tyranny or domination by a minority, and responsiveness to unmet or changing needs among its citizens. Pluralist theory has the virtue of explaining how a political system can handle both of these problems simultaneously. To the extent that the American political system approximates the pluralist model, it is argued, it will produce regular and orderly change with the consent of the governed.

Those who support this interpretation are not unaware of urban riots and the considerable history of violent conflict in the United States. However, they tend to view such events as abnormalities or pathologies arising from the gap between an always imperfect reality and an ideal, abstract model. In other words, the occasional, admitted failures of American democracy to produce orderly change are caused by departures from the ideal conditions of pluralism. Furthermore, even a well-functioning thermostat sometimes produces temperatures that are momentarily too hot or too cold as it goes about giving us the proper temperature.

There is a vast literature on pluralism and the American political system, and the discussion here will not attempt to do it full justice. A particularly coherent and convincing statement of the case is made in Dahl's *Pluralist Democracy in the United States* (1967). Now Dahl is no mindless celebrator of the genius of American politics; he paints his subject with all its warts and blemishes. But the important point is that this darker side of American politics is viewed as blemish and not as the essence of his subject.

Dahl suggests (p. 24) that the "fundamental axiom in the theory and practice of American pluralism is . . . this: Instead of a single center of sovereign power there must be multiple centers of power, none of which is or can be wholly sovereign." Why is this so important? Because the "existence of multiple centers of power . . . will help to tame power, to secure the consent of all, and to settle conflicts peacefully."

The brilliance of pluralist thinking is illustrated by its ability to handle multiple problems simultaneously — the prevention of dominance by a single group or individual, responsiveness to the needs of its citizens, and the prevention of extreme or violent conflict. It deals with two very different threats to the political system. The first threat is that the delicate balance of competition will be destroyed by a temporarily ascendant group that will use its ascendancy to crush its competitors. The second threat is that in the stalemate of veto groups and countervailing power there will be ineffective government, leading to an accumulation of discontent that will destroy the legitimacy and threaten the stability of the existing system.

We can examine the pluralist answer by addressing the question of how an ideal pluralist system functions. To operate properly, pluralist political institutions require an underlying pluralist social structure and values as well. More specifically, the following conditions should prevail:

Procedural Consensus

There is acceptance of the "culture" of constitutional democracy. One operates within the rules, the rules are considered generally fair, and defeats are accepted because of the strong legitimacy attached to the manner of resolving conflicts. Dahl goes even further than procedural consensus and argues for a good deal of substantive consensus as well. "In the United States, there is a massive convergence of attitudes on a number of key issues that divide citizens in other countries. As one result, ways of life are not seriously threatened by the policies of opponents" (Dahl, p. 326).

Cross-Cutting Solidarities

Individuals have strong identifications and affiliations with solidarity groups at different levels below the total society — primary group, community, formal organization, religious group, ethnic group, social class, and so forth. Furthermore, these solidarities overlap and cut across each other in a complex web which creates multiple memberships linking individuals with different sets of others.

Open Access to the Political Arena

There are no barriers to a group getting a hearing. Dissatisfied groups are encouraged to translate their dissatisfaction into political demands, to find coalition partners among other powerful groups, and to create political reforms which remedy the unsatisfactory conditions. As Dahl argues (p. 24): "Because even minorities are provided with opportunities to veto solutions they strongly object to, the consent of all will be won in the long run." The political institutions offer multiple points at which to pursue one's demands. "The institutions . . . offer organized minorities innumerable sites in which to fight, perhaps to defeat, at any rate to damage an opposing coalition" (Dahl, p. 329).

Balance of Power or Countervailing Power Operation

There is a sufficiently large number of groups that no one group can dominate. Coalitions are fluid and impermanent, being formed more or less *de novo* for each issue or, at least, for each class of issues. Furthermore, issues partition groups in different ways so that many groups not in a present coalition are potential coalition partners on subsequent issues. "Because one center of power is set against another," Dahl writes (p. 24), "power itself will be tamed, civilized, controlled, and limited to decent human purposes, while coercion, the most evil form of power, will be reduced to a minimum."

When a political system meets these assumptions, it is argued, neither tyranny nor rigidity will result. No group will become dominant for several reasons. First, it will exercise self-restraint in exploiting any temporary ascendancy for normative reasons. The institutions will "generate politicians who learn how to deal gently with opponents, who struggle endlessly in building and holding coalitions together, who doubt the possibilities of great change, who seek compromises" (Dahl, p. 329). Thus, the political process encourages a normative commitment to a set of rules which would be violated by dealing too ruthlessly with an opponent.

Second, self-restraint is encouraged by long-run self-interest. In a world of constantly shifting coalitions, it is feckless to antagonize groups which may be tomorrow's allies on some other set of issues. Third, self-restraint is encouraged by short-run self-interest. Because of the nature of cross-cutting solidarities, any temporarily ascendant group is likely to include many members who *also* belong to those groups who might be the victims of the abuse of power. In such a situation, any efforts to use power to injure or to destroy the power of opponents are automatically threats to the *internal stability* of the groups that would attempt such action. Such efforts stimulate factionalism and costly division within the ranks.

Finally, if self-restraint is not sufficient, efforts to achieve domination will encourage neutral and uninvolved groups to join an opposing coalition which controls greater resources than the temporarily ascendant group or coalition. Power which threatens to get out of hand stimulates countervailing power.

Many of the same pluralist conditions help to produce responsiveness as well. The critical element in this argument is that in the normal operation of the political system dissatisfied groups are encouraged to organize and translate their dissatisfaction into concrete political demands. Several elements in the political system lead to such encouragement. First, competitive elections assure that political parties will woo dissatisfied groups that have achieved some degree of strength, either to broaden their base of support or to prevent the allegiance of such groups to their competitors. Second, existing interest groups with similar or overlapping interests will facilitate organizations of such dissatisfied groups, seeing in them new allies. Third, multiple points of access to the political system will encourage participation by making available many sites for possible influence. Fourth, such organization and participation will be encouraged by the normative commitment of existing competitors to open access.

Thus, no group will long remain unrepresented, and it will find its entry into the political arena smoothed and facilitated by powerful allies who find it useful to do so for their own purposes. There will be no need for such groups to violate the existing rules of democratic politics to bring about the remedy of legitimate grievances.

The American political system, in this argument, approximates the underlying pluralist social structure and values quite closely. The result is an image of American politics as a contest carried out under well-defined rules. The rules prohibit the use of violence or any efforts aimed at permanently removing other contestants from the game. The essence of the competition is bargaining for relative advantage with the attendant tactics of influence trading, coalition formation, logrolling and the like.

It is a game that any number can play. The only rule of entry is that the contesting group must agree to behave itself. More specifically, this means that it must honor the rights of the existing participants by not striving to destroy them or to render them permanently impotent, and it must not be too unruly in its means. Contestants who misbehave are excluded from the contest by general agreement. Subject only to this broadest of restrictions, all are welcome to come in and try their luck.

This, then, is the essence of the pluralist image. It is the product of a subtle and persuasive argument with roots going back to James Madison and extending through an array of subsequent political theorists. In suggesting its inadequacies and in exploring an alternative image, I intend no denial of the great intellectual insights into the workings of political systems in general, and of American politics in particular, that we owe to this body of thought.

FLAWS IN THE PLURALIST HEAVEN

"The flaw in the pluralist heaven," writes Schattschneider (1960, p. 35), "is that the heavenly chorus sings with a strong upper-class accent. Probably about 90 percent of the people cannot get into the pressure system." In one form or another, this theme is present in most writing that is critical of pluralist theory.

One line of criticism of the pluralist image of American politics challenges its argument about the lack of dominance by a single center of power. This theme is given classical expression in Mills' *The Power Elite* (1956). Mills argues for the existence of a level of power operation not touched by pluralist assumptions. The pluralist model, Mills grants, is applicable to a middle level of power, but a series of really major decisions are dominated by a small group which is not subject to the constraints operating at the middle level.

Mills' argument is vulnerable at a number of points, in large part because of his emphasis on the issue of dominance rather than responsiveness. As Pilisuk and Hayden argue (1965, p. 78): "Where Mills' theory is most awkward is in his assertions that the elite can, and does, make its decisions against the will of others and regardless of external conditions. . . . What is attributed to the elite is a rather fantastic quality: literal omnipotence." Pilisuk and Hayden attempt to remedy this weakness in Mills while preserving his major insights by making the argument (p. 92) in more sophisticated, institutional terms rather than in terms of a "ruling group."

> In the United States there is no ruling group. . . . Nor is there any easily discernible ruling institutional order, so meshed have the separate sources of elite power become. But there is a social structure which is organized to create and protect power centers with only partial accountability. . . . We are describing the current system as one of overall "minimal accountability" and "minimal consent." We mean that the role of democratic review, based on popular consent, is made marginal and reactive. Elite groups are minimally accountable to publics and have a substantial, though by no means maximum, freedom to shape popular attitudes.

Having argued for the imbeddedness of a military-industrial complex in mainstream American institutions and mores, they conclude that "Our concept is not that American society contains a ruling military-industrial complex. Our concept is more nearly that American society *is* a military-industrial complex" (p. 98).

Some of this criticism can simply be accepted by pluralists by recasting it in different language. Concentration of power is necessary, it can be argued, to enjoy the fruits of leadership. Where substantial consensus exists on goals, many issues reflect technical problems. Agger, Goldrich, and Swanson write (1964, p. 76): "Pluralists take the position, specifically or implicitly, that . . . major decisional options are not shaped by an influential ruling elite so much as they are by 'technical' factors which, assuming there is a desire for 'functional rationality,' would lead rational men to similar choice situations or decisional outcomes, regardless of socio-economic class or official positions."

If the collective interest is to be served, then the social system needs specialists in goal attainment to exercise disproportionate influence on its behalf (cf. Parsons, 1960). In this view, to see such essential leadership functions as "undemocratic" in some way is to impose an ideology on an essential fact of social life: concentration of power is necessary for efficient goal attainment. Many social scientists sympathetic to the pluralist argument probably share the view which Dahl (1961, p. 321) attributes to members of the political stratum. "Public involvement may seem undesirable . . . for alterations in the prevailing norms are often subtle matters, better obtained by negotiation than by the crudities and over-simplifications of public debate."

This defense of pluralism is, I believe, an important one, but it deals with only one part of the attack. I share the suspicions of the critics of pluralism that it is a partial truth that misses or blurs certain problems and paints an overly sanguine picture of the operation of power in American society. However, my own discomfort, like that of Pilisuk and Hayden, is not with the assertions about the absence of a small power elite or ruling group.

The pluralist interpretation seems more vulnerable and in need of modification on the issue of permeability and openness to efforts at change. "Groups provide a great deal of necessary social efficiency," Lowi writes (1971, p. 5). "They are effective means of articulating and representing interests and providing low-level social controls that reduce the need for governmental coercion. But the very success of established groups is a mortgage against a future of new needs that are not yet organized or are not readily accommodated by established groups."

From time to time, previously unorganized groups begin to find a political voice. Vague dissatisfactions begin to crystallize over some more specific claim or demand for change, be it incremental or revolutionary. These challenging groups vary in the responses they experience. Some collapse quickly without leaving a visible mark, some are destroyed by attack, some have their programs preempted by competitors, some are given the formal trappings of influence without its substance, some die and rise again from the ashes, some shove their way, yelling and screaming, into the political arena and become permanent fixtures, some walk in on the arm of well-placed sponsors, and some wander in unnoticed and remain in by fait accompli.

It is one task of any interpretation of American politics to explain the varied experience of these challenging groups. The pluralist interpretation provides one such explanation:

1.   Only those groups whose objectives leave intact pluralist social structure and values will be "successful." Participation and success is denied to those who attack and try to change the pluralist order itself.

2.   Only those groups which use institutionally provided means will be successful — in particular, the electoral system and the political pressure or lobbying system. Those who resort to the tactics of the streets will be unsuccessful.

Part of the task of this book will be to explore the adequacy of this pluralist answer. But as we attempt to understand the careers of challenging groups, we will go beyond the answer above to explore many variables where precise relevance for the pluralist argument may not be clear. Ultimately, the concern here is to make sense of the experience of challenging groups in America, not simply to evaluate the particular pluralist answer. But pluralist theory provides the logical starting point for this quest.

In Chapter Two, I will clarify what is included and excluded by the term "challenging group" and will introduce the 53 challenging groups which form the basis of this study. In Chapter Three, measures of the outcome of challenges will be discussed as we try to come to terms with the elusive concept of success or failure. In Chapter Four, the nature of the challenging group's objectives will be related to outcomes. In Chapter Five, we will explore the theory of public goods and its implications for the ability of challenging groups to mobilize their constituency. In Chapter Six, the means of influence used will become the central theme. In Chapter Seven, the focus will shift to the internal organization of the challenging group. In Chapter Eight, some assessment of the influence of different historical contexts will be attempted. Finally, in Chapter Nine, I will suggest what I think is the overall thrust of this collection of results and its implications for our image of the permeability of the American political arena.

REFERENCES

Agger, Robert; Goldrich, Daniel; and Swanson, Bert E. *The Rulers and the Ruled.* New York: Wiley, 1964.

Dahl, Robert. *Who Governs?* New Haven: Yale University Press, 1961.

_____. *Pluralist Democracy in the United States: Conflict and Consent.* Chicago: Rand-McNally, 1967.

Galenson, Walter. *The CIO Challenge to the AFL.* Cambridge, Mass.: Harvard University Press, 1960.

Gamson, William A. "Stable Unrepresentation in American Society." *American Behavioral Scientist,* 12 November/December 1968.

Lowi, Theodore. *The Politics of Disorder.* New York: Basic Books, 1971.

Mills, C. Wright. *The Power Elite.* New York: Oxford University Press, 1956.

Parsons, Talcott. "The Distribution of Power in American Society." T. Parsons (ed.), *Structure and Process in Modern Societies.* New York: Free Press, 1960.

Pilisuk, Marc, and Hayden, Thomas. "Is There a Military Industrial Complex Which Prevents Peace?" *Journal of Social Issues,* 21 July 1965.

Quint, Howard H. *The Forging of American Socialism: Origins of the Modern Movement.* Indianapolis: Bobbs-Merrill, 1964.

Schattschneider, E. E. *The Semi-Sovereign People.* New York: Holt, Rinehart, and Winston, 1960.

Sweeney, Vincent D. *The United Steelworkers of America,* 1956.

chapter two

The Challenging Group

The actor whose political career will concern us is the carrier of a challenge to the political system. It is usually a formal organization although the degree of "formality" may vary a great deal. To be a member of a challenging group may involve no more than a psychological commitment as with "membership" in the Democratic or Republican Party. With others it may involve a set of concrete acts including blood oaths and other rituals. Formal or informal, the organization has a name which it has taken for itself or been given by others.[1] Most important for our purposes, it is an entity capable of taking action — of holding meetings, planning, issuing statements, calling demonstrations, and raising money.

It will help us to understand the nature of a challenging group by distinguishing among three distinct concepts of a "target" for such groups: (1) the target of influence, (2) the target of mobilization, and (3) the target of benefits. A target of *influence* is that set of individuals, groups, or social institutions that must alter their decisions or policies in order for a challenging group to correct a situation to which it objects. Such a target is the object of actual or planned influence attempts by the group, called here the group's

---

[1] Challenging groups are similar to what Zald and Ash (1966) call "social movement organizations."

14

antagonist. In the case of the Steel Workers Organizing Committee, for example, the various steel companies were the antagonist. In the case of the Social Revolutionary Clubs (Anarcho-Communists), the national regime was the antagonist. In the case of an electoral party challenger a set of political offices or officeholders are the relevant antagonists.

The targets of *mobilization* are those individuals or groups whose resources and energy the group seeks in carrying out its efforts at change, called here the group's *constituency*. To make this clear, it is necessary to deal with an important ambiguity in the concept of political mobilization. The concept of mobilization embraces two closely related ideas, the activation of commitment and the creation of commitment. The *activation* of commitment involves efforts to move those who already possess some degree of commitment to take a specific action. For example, the American Medical Association may urge its members to get on the telephone to their Congressmen to oppose the passage of Medicare legislation, or a union may urge its members to oppose the re-election of someone they regard as antilabor.

The *creation* of commitment means a change from a low generalized readiness to act to a high generalized readiness to act collectively. A group with a high readiness to act requires a minimal amount of effort to convince them to act on a given occasion. A small precipitating event or a mere public call to action by trusted leaders is enough to produce a full response by a constituency in a high state of readiness. A group with a low readiness to act may not respond even to a much greater effort to have them engage in a specific action.

The term "mobilization" is often used to refer to both of the above processes without distinction. Here, I will use it strictly to refer to the creation of commitment, saving the term "activation" for efforts to get supporters of varying degrees of commitment to take specific actions. Mobilization is a process of increasing the readiness to act collectively by building the loyalty of a constituency to an organization or to a group of leaders. Activation is part of an influence attempt; mobilization is part of an organizing process that precedes specific efforts at influence.

The constituency of a group, then, is that set of individuals whose *readiness* to participate in collective action the group is attempting to increase. This typically takes the form of enlisting such individuals as members of an organization, but it need not require this and frequently involves more than this. For the Steel Workers Organizing Committee, the constituency consisted of those steel workers employed by plants the group was attempting to organize. For a revolutionary group, the constituency might be industrial workers or some other group whose class consciousness the group is attempting to build. In the case of an electoral challenger, the constituency is that portion of the electorate from whom the group hopes to win support.

The target of *benefits* are those individuals or groups whom the challenging group hopes will be affected positively by the changes that it seeks from its antagonist. I will call this target the group's *beneficiary*. There are many cases in which the beneficiary of the group and its constituency are identical, but this is not always true. In some cases, the changes will affect everyone more or less equally whether they are members of the group's constituency or not. In other cases, the constituency and beneficiary may have little overlap. In the case of the Steel Workers Organizing Committee, for example, the constituency and the beneficiary were identical—in both cases, the steel workers. In the case of the American Committee for the Outlawry of War, the policy changes which the group sought would not affect its middle-class reform constituency anymore than anyone else. In the case of an abolitionist group, the intended beneficiaries were the slaves, slave owners, and the society as a whole but not the nonslave holding constituency of the movement in particular.

The issue of a group's beneficiary will become relevant in Chapter Five when we explore how the relationship between constituency and beneficiary affects success. For defining a challenging group, only the antagonist and the constituency are relevant. A challenging group meets two central criteria:

1. *It must be seeking the mobilization of an unmobilized constituency.* Established interest groups are hereby excluded even though they may be seeking changes. A group is no longer a challenging group once it can call upon an already mobilized constituency whenever it decides to attempt influence. Even established groups, of course, make continued efforts to maintain the commitment of their members and express concern about membership "apathy." The practical issue, then, is a matter of a degree —whether a group faces as a central and primary task the mobilization of a constituency where it does not initially exist, or whether

this is a secondary task centered mainly on the maintenance of a commitment that threatens to decay without efforts at continual renewal. Only a group in the former situation qualifies as a challenging group.

A newly-formed group that is so rich in resources from the start that it has no need to mobilize a constituency is also excluded. For example, a group of influential citizens who formed an ad hoc group to block the passage of a treaty in the Senate would not be included unless it saw the need to draw in and mobilize an underlying constituency before it could exert effective influence. To the extent that the members hoped to rely on the persuasiveness of their arguments or the prestige of the names on their letterhead, they would lack the focus on mobilization as a primary task.

2. *Its antagonist lies outside of its constituency.* Those groups whose target of influence is a subset of their constituency are not defined as challenging groups. A utopian community, for example, attempting to mobilize a constituency to participate in a better way of life, is not included. It would be included if its plans required it to obtain new legislation or the abandonment of certain governmental policies since these objectives imply outside antagonists. Similarly, a messianic group would be excluded if it offered the members salvation by altering their own way of life without the necessity of influencing outsiders. A benevolent association, hoping to provide certain services for members, or a fraternal order, dedicated to performing acts of charity, would be similarly excluded. In short, challenging groups seek influence beyond what their constituency has the power to implement on its own; they must gain concessions or the actual offices and authority of nonmembers to achieve their goals.

Beyond these primary criteria, we have adopted a number of more or less arbitrary conventions to put practical boundaries around the universe of challenging groups we will consider in this study. Only those groups that surfaced in the United States from 1800 to 1945 are included. Contemporary groups are excluded because in many cases these challenges are still in process, and we cannot yet state what their outcome is. Because we are concerned primarily with societal power relations, we include only those challenging groups with a constituency extending beyond the borders of a single state. The group itself may be based in a single state, but its constituency cannot also be so confined. Given the dispersion of its constituency, the changes sought by the group cannot be implemented by action in a single, limited locale. This has the effect of eliminating from the universe of challenging groups considered here a vast number of small challenges directed, for example, at a single municipality or state government. It does not exclude groups with a constituency in several states whose local supporters are making essentially similar demands for change in their respective cities.

We also exclude groups whose members are neither American citizens nor striving for such citizenship. In particular, we do not include the various Indian nations, which have engaged in numerous wars and conflicts with the federal government, as challenging groups.

We also exclude groups whose constituency consists only or primarily of other organizations. Thus, many federations are excluded because they do not directly try to mobilize individuals. An association or watchdog for existing groups, designed to coordinate their efforts or monitor and influence others on their behalf, is not considered a challenging group. However, many groups which are *formally* federations in fact attempt to mobilize individuals on behalf of broader goals than their member organizations are able or willing to pursue. Such groups—the American Federation of Labor, for example—qualify as challenging groups. They have different protagonists than the member organizations and attempt to mobilize and build the loyalty of individuals to the federation by pursuit of their own, complementary objectives.

A challenging group that began as a faction or splinter from an existing group qualifies if it meets the basic criteria, but only if it establishes an independent operating structure. A faction that is challenging the leadership does not qualify unless it is both a separate organizational entity and has an antagonist outside of the organization of which it is part. Challenges by insurgent groups within an organization, aimed at changing that organization or seizing power within it, are not included here.

Satellites of other groups are excluded when they are merely a part of a parent organization. For example, a ladies' auxiliary, a vigilante protection unit, an operating committee within the group, a caucus, an advertising bureau, and the like are not treated as independent challenges when they have no separate cause and are merely providing some service or reinforcement for the parent group.

THE SAMPLE OF CHALLENGING GROUPS

The universe of groups that this book addresses are all those challenging groups that surfaced in American society between 1800 and 1945. The members of this universe meet the primary criteria: they are seeking the mobilization of an unmobilized constituency and their antagonist or target of influence lies outside of this constituency. We have restricted or clarified this universe further by adopting conventions dealing with the geographical breadth of the constituency, citizenship status, federations, splinter groups, and satellites.

There have been between five and six hundred challenging groups in American society that meet the criteria described here. We will focus on a sample of 53 of them. Shortly, I intend to defend the claim that these 53 groups are an equal probability sample of the defined universe of challenging groups in American society. But first, it will be useful if the reader has at least a general descriptive sense of the variety and nature of the members of the sample.

The 53 challengers range from the narrowest of reform groups to the most sweeping of revolutionary groups. One group, the League of American Wheelmen, aimed only at the modest goal of eliminating a series of restrictions on the use of the bicycle and winning the right to ride on public highways. Later, flushed by success, their ambitions grew to include as well the improvement of public highways as they became participants in the "good roads movement." In contrast to these most finite of goals, the German-American Bund hoped to do no less than remodel the American political system along the lines of German National Socialism.

Some groups—for example, the American Association of University Professors—have such a respectable image today that they constitute an embarrassment to a book on social protest. Others—for example, the Tobacco Night Riders of the black patch area of Kentucky and Tennessee—look more disreputable by contemporary standards than they probably did at the time. But, then, even the most reputable of groups today was usually not considered such during its period of challenge.

Some of the 53 are famous and well-remembered—for example, Father Coughlin's National Union for Social Justice. Others—for example, the League of Deliverance, a group that aimed at excluding Chinese labor from the United States—are remembered only by a handful of professional students of American labor and nativist movements.

Appendix A gives a brief description, including the period of challenge, of all 53 groups. We can divide them into four broad, descriptive categories. Twenty of the groups (38 percent) were occupationally based. The most obvious examples are unions of blue collar workers—for example, The Packinghouse Workers Organizing Committee and the American Labor Union, a forerunner of the International Workers of the World or "Wobblies." But the category also includes middle-class occupational groups (The American Federation of Teachers), craftsmen (The Union Trade Society of Journeymen Tailors and The National Brotherhood of Baseball Players), and farm organizations (The Tobacco Night Riders and the Dairymen's League).

Seventeen of the groups (32 percent) were one form or another of a "reform group." Some of these groups—for example, the American Anti-Slavery Society, a leading abolitionist group—were considered very radical in their day. Some—for example, Theodore Roosevelt's Bull Moose Party and William Randolph Hearst's Independence League—were conventional political parties seeking electoral success. Some—for example, A. Philip Randolph's March on Washington Committee and the National Urban League—were civil rights groups. Some—for example, the Church Peace Union and the American Committee for the Outlawry of War—were peace groups. Some—for example, the Federal Suffrage Association and the American Proportional Representation League—sought specific institutional reforms in one area.

Ten of the groups (19 percent) were rooted in the socialist tradition. The sample includes the granddaddy of socialism in America, The International Workingmen's Association, or First International. Some of the socialist groups—for example, the National Student League—were campus-based. Some—for example, the Progressive Labor Party—were electorally oriented; while others —for example, the Revolutionary Workers League—strongly rejected the possibility of effecting change through the ballot box.

Finally, six of the groups (11 percent) were some variety of right-wing or nativist group. Electoral challengers—for example, the Native American or American Republican Party—are included here along with such classical right-wing challengers as the Christian Front against Communism and the German-American Bund. The distribution of the 53 groups is summarized in Figure 2–1.

FIGURE 2–1
Distribution of Types of Groups in the Sample

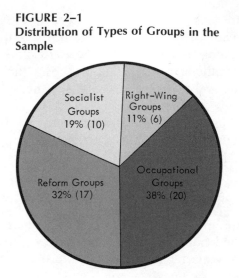

FIGURE 2–2
Distribution of Challenging Groups by Decade of Origin

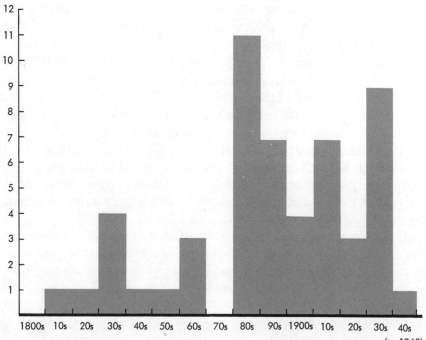

The groups are also well distributed over time. A little over half (55 percent) began their careers in the 19th century, and every single decade except 1800–1810 and the 1870s is represented by at least one new challenger. Figure 2–2 shows the distribution of groups by decade and reveals the 1880s and the 1930s as the most productive of new challenges with the 1910s and 1890s not far behind. The 1830s are the major contributor in the pre-civil war period. The median length of a challenge period is about eight years, but there is great variability.

THE SAMPLING PROCEDURE

The 53 groups are a representative sample of all challenging groups, as defined here, in American society between 1800 and 1945. It is no easy matter to get an equal probability sample since no list or sampling frame exists. Such a list must be created with a considerable investment of effort and expense.

Why bother? Why not simply pick groups that are well-documented and that have various relevant characteristics? Why not pick interesting groups instead of giving such trivial efforts as the Society for the Promotion of Manual Labor in Literary Institutions the same probability for inclusion as the Ku Klux Klan or the Wobblies? Surely the resources of this study would have been more usefully allocated if these latter groups had been included at the expense of the former?

The answer is simply that we can learn a great deal more from an unbiased sample than from a biased one. The central issues concern the permeability of the political arena by new participants and how their success or failure is influenced by their strategy and organization. There are two obvious biases in picking well-documented or "interesting" groups. First, we are likely to encounter a heavy bias toward success, toward groups that lasted. Those that have made it inspire histories, indeed, sometimes even sponsor them. Those that collapse are not around to enlighten would-be chroniclers.

Of course, some groups that have "failed" do inspire historians, and this brings us to a second bias. Groups that have had an especially dramatic life, that have been involved in violent clashes and have produced martyrs, are likely to be remembered. Leftist groups, because they attract intellectuals as participants, are more likely to be written about after their demise. Thus, there is every reason to suspect that a sample of interesting failures will be quite unrepresentative of unsuccessful groups. Beyond these predictable biases, many other, more subtle biases would probably be operating as well, misleading us in our interpretations of what we might find.

By working with a representative sample of challenging groups, we minimize these biases. There are, as I will discuss later, certain problems with what is included in the *universe* of challenging groups, but at least we can be confident that the 53 groups in the sample represent this defined universe reasonably well.

Appendix B contains a detailed description of the procedure for compiling the sampling frame, and I will only summarize the main elements here. We began by compiling a *gross* list of potential sample entries. This gross list was as exhaustive as possible, but we were not concerned ' with how many invalid entries were included. We accepted the fact that most of the entries would, on investigation, turn out not to meet our criteria for a challenging group.

The gross list was based on the indexes of general and specialized histories. A coder turned to the index of each source used and recorded the name of each formal organization and each collective behavior episode mentioned (e.g., "Shays' Rebellion" or "The Watts Riot"). High reliabilities were achieved between independent coders using this procedure.

We began the list with general sources—for example, Louis Filler's *A Dictionary of Social Reform*—and proceeded to a bibliography of about 75 books covering different types of potential challenging groups. That our bibliographic categories overlapped was of no concern, but it was necessary that every challenging group fall into at least one of the following types: agricultural, labor, ethnic, women, religious, prohibition, nativist, reform, professional, business and commerce, conservation, black, socialist, peace, veterans, rightist, and radical left groups. Many of the sources used were quite specialized—for example, Hicks and Saloutos, *Agricultural Discontent in the Middle West*.

For each book, an index of new entries was compiled—that is, the percentage of total entries in the source not already included in the file. Initially, we established a criterion of completeness that three consecutive books from different categories should yield less than 20 percent new entries. In fact, we exceeded this substantially, and the final *dozen* sources were all below 20 percent, averaging about 10 percent new entries. The new entries were not necessarily challenging groups, of course, but were merely additional names of organizations or collective behavior episodes. It is a reasonable guess that a lower percentage of these new entries were challenging groups since many appeared to be highly localized groups—for example, chapters or branches of organizations already included. To check this possibility, we examined the final 20 new entries, and none turned out to be a challenging group (see Appendix B for details).

Once we were satisfied with the completeness of the frame, we drew a sample.[2] Each card in the gross file had 11 chances in 100 of being selected, and we ended up with a total of 467 entries. We then investigated each entry to determine whether or not it met the criteria for a challenging group. Most did not and were discarded; in fact, we were left with only 64 or 14 percent of the original cards. Note, however, that these 64 were representative of all the valid cards in the gross file even though we could not identify those that did not fall into the sample.

Of these 64 valid entries, we were able to get reasonably complete information on 53 of them, a response rate of 83 percent. Of the other 11, it is entirely possible that some would not qualify —for example, the Philadelphia Journeymen House Painters Association—but, in the absence of more conclusive evidence to question their validity, we assume that they meet the definition of a challenging group. In this sense, the figure of an 83 percent response rate is a conservative one and might turn out to be higher if we were to uncover new information on them. The 11 missing groups are described in Appendix B.

THE NATURE OF THE DATA

A series of identical questions were asked about each challenging group (see Appendix C). Instead of employing our questionnaire to interview individuals as one would on a survey, we employed it to interview books and documents. We experienced our own equivalent of the respondent who is never at home or slams the door in one's face—the group that left no record of its adventures.

Whenever possible, we relied on existing professional histories,

---

[2] The sample was actually drawn in a series of waves, but this has no importance for the discussion here.

turning to primary sources only when we were forced to by gaps in our information. Special library collections such as the University of Michigan's Labadie Collection proved very helpful in some difficult cases, particularly with left-wing groups. For most groups several different sources were used, with biases duly noted. A complete list of sources used is included in the bibliography and the reference sections of this book.

The compiler used the questionnaire to complete a "protocol" on each challenging group, a process requiring an average of 80 hours per protocol. For each question, the compiler gave a short summary of the (sometimes contradictory) answers found in the several sources used. He or she then included a photocopy of the relevant paragraphs or pages from the sources bearing on the particular question. If a section was relevant to more than one question, it was appropriately cross-referenced.

To illustrate, in response to the question, "To what extent were challenging group members subject to arrest?" the compiler of the Christian Front against Communism noted the following: "There were 233 criminal prosecutions due to racial clashes in 1939 in New York alone, and 17 Brooklyn Fronters were arrested for conspiring to overthrow the government." These comments were followed by photocopies of fairly lengthy descriptions from two sources concerning the circumstances of these arrests and indictments.

The basic questionnaire is included in Appendix C. Each question had a series of additional instructions to the compiler concerning the type of information being sought. For example, the compiler was asked to note any evidence on whether arrests were isolated and sporadic, or patterned and repetitive, and to note any evidence relating to official sanction and justification of arrests. For each protocol, the compiler established certain time reference points related to major events in the group's history and was asked to note, whenever possible, the relationship of the answers to these time points — for example, "arrests occurred from Time 1 to Time 4 but not after Time 4."

The questionnaire contained sections on the group's interaction with different institutional spheres — the law enforcement system, government agencies, mass media, political parties, legislative bodies, and private interest groups. Another section dealt with the internal characteristics of the challenging group — its leadership, organizational structure, resources, tactics, ideology, and so forth.

The final section of the questionnaire dealt with the outcome of the group's challenge, the central topic of the next chapter.

Once the protocols were completed, codes were developed for each section. Because our information was often quiet spotty, we relied heavily on quite simple codes. For example, in the case of arrests, our code basically asked whether group members were ever arrested or not.[3] Given such simple codes, it is probably not surprising that coding reliability between independent coders averaged 92 percent. Reliabilities of this order were sometimes achieved by combining categories in which independent coders were unable to make reliable distinctions. For example, if the code for arrests had included categories of "none," "a few," and "many," it might have turned out that no disagreements between coders occurred between "none" and "a few" but that several occurred between "a few" and "many." In such an instance, if reliability was below a criterion of 80 percent, we would have combined the unreliable categories to produce a 100 percent reliable code containing only the categories "none" and "some."

We also employed a variety of checks on the quality of the protocols. For several groups, protocols were completed independently by different compilers and the results checked. It was then possible to see if coders using independent versions of a protocol for the same group obtained essentially similar results.

Through these various efforts at controlling the quality of our data, we were able to keep our demands on it within reasonable limits. In many cases, we wished to measure things that were beyond what the protocols could reliably yield. Where this occurred, we learned to live with the frustration of not measuring some variable of interest rather than attempting to extract gold from inferior ore. Hopefully, the information that we were able to extract, gross as it sometimes is, is of sufficient interest in its own right to ease the frustration of not being able to satiate our curiosity.

A FINAL CAVEAT

A central purpose of this research is to gain insight into the permeability of the American political system by different types of groups using various strategies. It is important to this objective that

---

[3] It also distinguished test cases deliberately initiated by the group from ordinary arrests.

we use a low threshold to identify a challenging group, lest we be left with nothing but a sample of highly visible successes. The procedure used employed a modest threshold but a threshold nonetheless. Ultimately, a group must have reached some point of activity even to attract the notice of an historian who was interested in groups of its special type.

There may be aggregates of individuals, very much outside of the political arena and suffering some form of social disadvantage, that never organize enough to stage a hostile outburst or form a protest group. Clearly, such quasi-groups or potential groups elude our net of challenging groups. Yet, their inability to mount a challenge may be an extremely important datum for interpreting the American political experience. Some groups may be so far outside that their cries or curses never reach our ears, if indeed they are ever uttered. We will have nothing to say here about such potential challenging groups. I don't know in what numbers they exist, if at all. This book will shed no light on them. But their possible existence must be remembered in any conclusions about the openness of the American political system we hope to draw from a study of actual challenging groups.

REFERENCE

Zald, Mayer N., and Ash, Roberta. "Social Movement Organizations: Growth, Decay, and Change." *Social Forces*, March 1966, 44:327–41.

chapter three

The Meaning of Success

Success is an elusive idea. What of the group whose leaders are honored or rewarded while their supposed beneficiaries linger in the same cheerless state as before? Is such a group more or less successful than another challenger whose leaders are vilified and imprisoned even as their program is eagerly implemented by their oppressor? Is a group a failure if it collapses with no legacy save inspiration to a generation that will soon take up the same cause with more tangible results? And what do we conclude about a group that accomplishes exactly what it set out to achieve and then finds its victory empty of real meaning for its presumed beneficiaries? Finally, we must add to these questions the further complications of groups with multiple antagonists and multiple areas of concern. They may achieve some results with some targets and little or nothing with others.

It is useful to think of success as a set of outcomes, recognizing that a given challenging group may receive different scores on equally valid, different measures of outcome. These outcomes fall into two basic clusters: one concerned with the fate of the challenging group as an organization and one with the distribution of new advantages to the group's beneficiary. The central issue in the first cluster focuses on the *acceptance* of a challenging group by its antagonists as a valid spokesman for a legitimate set of interests. The central issue in the second cluster focuses on whether the group's beneficiary gains *new advantages* during the challenge and its aftermath.

Both of these outcome clusters require elaboration, but, for the moment, consider each as if it were a single, dichotomous variable. Assume a group that has a single antagonist and a single act which they wish this antagonist to perform—for example, a reform group which desires a particular piece of national legislation. We ask of such a group, did its antagonist accept it as a valid spokesman for the constituency that it was attempting to mobilize or did it deny such acceptance? Secondly, did the group gain the advantages it sought—for example, the passage of the legislation that it desired?

By combining these two questions, as in Figure 3–1, we acquire four possible outcomes: full response, co-optation, preemption, and collapse. The full response and collapse categories are relatively unambiguous successes and failures—in the one case the achievement of both acceptance and new advantages, in the other, the achievement of neither. The remainder are mixed categories: co-optation is the term used for acceptance without new advantages and preemption for new advantages without acceptance.

FIGURE 3–1
Outcome of Resolved Challenges

| | | *Acceptance* | |
		Full	None
New	Many	Full response	Preemption
Advantages	None	Co-optation	Collapse

Figure 3–1 is the paradigm for handling outcomes of challenging groups, but it requires additional complexity before it can be used to handle as diverse a set of groups as the 53 represented here. Acceptance must be given a special meaning for revolutionary groups, for example, which seek not a nod of recognition from an antagonist but its destruction and replacement. Similarly, new "advantages" are not always easy to define. We must deal with cases in which a group seeks, for example, relatively intangible value changes, shifts in the scope of authority, or a change in procedures as well as the simpler case of material benefits for a well-defined group.

THE ENDPOINT OF A CHALLENGE

The outcome measures used refer to "ultimate" outcome, to the state of the group at the end of its challenge. A given group might achieve significant new advantages at one point without receiving acceptance, but we would not consider that preemption had occurred as long as it continued to press an active challenge. Only when it eventually collapsed or ceased activity would we classify its outcome as preemption. Or, if it eventually won acceptance, its outcome would be full response instead. Similarly, the new advantages might be withdrawn and the group brutally crushed, making "collapse" the appropriate outcome. Thus, during its period of challenge, a group might appear to be in one or another cell of Figure 3–1 at different times, but the outcome measures only consider its location at the end.

A challenge period is considered over when one of the following occurs:

1. *The challenging group ceases to exist as a formal entity.* It may officially dissolve, declaring itself no longer in existence. Or, it may merge with another group, ceasing to maintain a separate identity. Note, however, that a group does not cease to exist by merely changing its name to refurbish its public image. Operationally, we consider that two names represent the same challenging group if and only if:

   a.   The major goals, purposes, and functions of the two groups are the same.
   b.   The constituency remains the same.
   c.   The average challenging group member and potential member would agree that the new-name group is essentially the old group relabeled.

2. *The challenging group, while not formally dissolving, ceases mobilization and influence activity.* A five-year period of inactivity is considered sufficient to specify the end of the challenge. If, after such a dormant period, the group becomes active again, it is considered a new challenging group in spite of its organizational continuity with the old challenger. This occurred, in fact, with two of the 53 challengers in the sample. In each case the period of dormancy was quite a bit longer than the required five years, and, in one case, the geographical location of activity was different as well.

Marking the end of a challenge is more difficult with groups that continue to exist and be active. The line between being a challenging group and an established interest group is not always sharp. The essential difference lies in how institutionalized a conflict relationship exists between the group and its antagonists. When this conflict becomes regulated and waged under some standard operating procedures, the challenge period is over. Operationally, this can be dated from the point at which the group is accepted. Hence, for continuing groups, the challenge period is over when:

3. *The challenging group's major antagonists accept the group as a valid spokesman for its constituency and deal with it as such.* In the case of unions, this is indicated by formal recognition of the union as a bargaining agent for the employees. In other cases, the act of acceptance is less clear, and, even in the case of unions, different companies extend recognition at different times. Issues such as these are dealt with in the discussion of measures of acceptance below.

With continuing groups, then, there is some inevitable arbitrariness in dating the end of a challenge. The compiler was instructed to err, in ambiguous cases, on the side of a later date. Thus, where acute conflict continues to exist between the group and important antagonists, the challenge is not considered over even when some other antagonists may have begun to deal with the challenger in a routinized way. Furthermore, by extending the challenge period, we include new benefits that might be excluded by using a premature termination date.

MEASURING OUTCOMES

Acceptance

Did the relationship between the challenging group and its antagonists change from the beginning to the end of the challenge? Although more than 75 percent of the groups here are more complicated, we will begin the discussion of this question with the simplest case of a group with a single antagonist. This antagonist necessarily begins with a relationship of active or passive hostility toward the challenging group or, at best, indifference. Acceptance involves a change from hostility or indifference to a more positive relationship.[1]

---

[1] If acceptance existed from the very beginning, the group would not qualify as a challenging group.

There are four indicators of this more positive relationship:

1.   *Consultation.* This must involve some degree of initiative by the antagonist. For example, if a legislative body has opened hearings on a matter of importance to the challenging group, the antagonist might invite representatives of the group to testify. On the other hand, if the group asks to testify and is permitted, this would not by itself be considered consultation. Similarly, if the antagonist issues a subpoena to force the group to testify, no consultation would be coded because the group is not being treated in such an instance as a legitimate spokesman for a constituency.

2.   *Negotiations.* If the antagonist is willing to enter into negotiations with the group on a continuing basis, not simply at the height of a particular crisis, this also implies acceptance of the group as a spokesman for a constituency. To be coded as acceptance, the negotiations must imply that the antagonist is dealing with the challenging group's negotiators as representatives of a constituency. The outcome of the negotiations is not relevant here; the two parties may fail to reach an acceptable settlement. But the mere fact of a continuing negotiating relationship implies acceptance.

3.   *Formal recognition.* This form of acceptance is characterized by the antagonist making explicit, typically in writing, that it recognizes the challenging group as a legitimate spokesman for a designated constituency. This is the functional equivalent of diplomatic recognition of a government in international politics. Nothing needs to be implied about general mutuality of interests or approval of the challenging group and its actions.

4.   *Inclusion.* This form of acceptance is characterized by the inclusion of challenging group leaders or members in positions of status or authority in the antagonist's organizational structure. It is essential, however, that the included challenging group members maintain their status, formally or informally, as group members. If serving in the antagonist's organization requires repudiating membership in the challenging group as a condition of office, it is not coded as acceptance through inclusion.

Special definitions of some of the above terms are needed to deal with certain types of groups. Consider, for example, revolutionary groups that have no desire for conventional acceptance by authorities they are attempting to overthrow. In such a case, only inclusion is a relevant measure of acceptance unless the group abandons its revolutionary ambitions. Inclusion, in this case, means self-inclusion. If the revolutionary group is successful, its members will be included at the expense of existing incumbents. In addition, the authority structure may be radically reorganized with old positions abolished and new ones created. Thus, acceptance does not imply psychological acceptance by the antagonist. A similar line of reasoning applies to electoral challenges. Here, the target is the set of offices being sought, and, again, only acceptance through inclusion is meaningful. Winning elections leads to such inclusion.

For a certain number of groups, the antagonist is not a circumscribed set of authorities but the general public. This is especially true with respect to groups that aim at changing values or aggregated individual practices. Many such groups — for example, the American Birth Control League — may also seek actions from targets such as a legislature or courts. But, when the "public" or "public opinion" is one target of change, how can acceptance be defined? The major consideration here is that acceptance refers to a response to the challenging group itself rather than to its issues or program. Thus, in the American Birth Control League example, the relevant consideration is not a change in attitudes toward contraception but toward the League that is promoting the change. There is an issue of acceptance only when the challenging group is initially regarded as deviant in some sense, either as subversive or as excessively eccentric. Acceptance in such a case is reflected by a change to the view that the organization is no longer deviant — that is, that a reasonable man or woman could belong to such a group and not be considered a crack-pot or worse.

Finally, we must consider the common situation of multiple antagonists. To handle this, targets are first grouped by types — for example, legislatures, steel companies, city governments, and so forth. Then, each type of antagonist is separately coded for a challenging group, allowing for distinctions in response within a given type between all, some, only one, and none. Thus, many groups have several types of antagonists and multiple codes for different kinds of acceptance for each.

This complex set of measures of acceptance must be reduced to some summary measures to be useful for analysis. I have explored several but will rely mostly on one very simple dichotomous one: the existence of a minimal acceptance relationship with *any* antagonist at the end of the challenge period. Such a relationship exists if there is a positive code on any of the measures of acceptance (consultation, negotiation, formal recognition, or inclusion) with any of the antagonists. Or, to put it the other way, a group without acceptance is one which has no type of acceptance from any antagonist.

I have chosen such an apparently minimal measure of acceptance because it it both unambiguous and, hence, highly reliable and also divides the sample quite neatly. Slightly more than half of the groups (28) never achieved even this minimal degree of acceptance; the other half (25) received one or another kind with some or all antagonists. In four cases, this involved nothing more than consultation, but, in the other 21, it involved one of the stronger forms of acceptance.

New Advantages

Did the potential beneficiaries of the challenging group receive what the group sought for them? No assumption is made that the challenging group necessarily caused the benefits. We asked only whether desired results were forthcoming, for whatever reason, during and immediately after the period of challenge.

In assessing the achievement of benefits, the group's own perspective and aspirations are the starting point. There are several cases in which I personally regarded the group's efforts at change as a form of false-consciousness. I do not believe, for example, that Father Coughlin's monetary nostrums would have actually helped the workers and farmers who were the alleged beneficiary of the National Union for Social Justice. There are even cases where a group began to question its own aspirations as it began to achieve them. The Grand Eight Hour Leagues, for example, successfully sought the passage of eight-hour legislation, but these laws turned out to be useless. And certainly many women today question the successful achievements of the Federal Suffrage Association, finding them a less meaningful accomplishment than the advocates of the time had expected. Similarly, the passage of the prohibition amendment failed to realize its advocates' hopes.

These reflections are intended as a caution in the interpretation of the achievement of new advantages. We leave it to the reader to judge whether the benefits were or would have been "real" benefits. They are benefits as defined by the challenging group. Some people, according to the challenging group, will improve their lot in life if certain things can be made to happen. If these desired changes occurred, then we regarded new advantages as having been realized, adopting the group's perspective on what constitutes a benefit.

Many of the 53 groups do not seek a specific material benefit but some broader change in institutions or values. Since no revolutions have occurred in American society during the period covered, it would appear that revolutionary groups are doomed to fail on this outcome measure. But it is not always clear just which group is or isn't revolutionary. It is consistent with some revolutionary ideologies, for example, to adopt immediate goals which are seen as providing benefits in their own right, as well as bringing one a step closer to Armageddon. If a so-called revolutionary group devotes energy and resources to the achievement of such an immediate goal, then different outcomes are possible as with any other group. The National Student League, for example, had general socialist goals, but it also concerned itself with a number of immediate campus issues, including the elimination of compulsory R.O.T.C. and the achievement of a free student press. If a group rejects all changes short of revolution and devotes its energy entirely to the mobilization process, then in this place and era, it will not have achieved new advantages.

For third-party challengers, new advantages are not measured by electoral success, which is used to measure acceptance, but by program enactment. Thus, a group may win some elections but fail to pass any significant legislation or otherwise influence policy (a case of co-optation); or it may fail to elect its own members but gain new advantages through the adoption of policy changes and programs by those who are elected (a case of preemption).

Similar reasoning applies to the challenging group that wishes to alter values or some aspect of public behavior. New advantages for the American Birth Control League, for example, meant a change in practice by Americans—increased usage of contraceptive techniques.[2] New advantages for the North Carolina Manumission Society are measured by their success in persuading individual plantation owners to grant freedom to their slaves. Note that in each of these cases, the target is still a target of change, not of mobilization.

How is the achievement of new advantages actually measured? First, consider the simplest case of a group with a single goal or area of concern. Four perceptions of goal achievement were

---

[2] New advantages can also come through changes in the legal status of birth control, another relevant goal of this particular challenging group.

coded: the perception of degree of achievement (1) by historians, (2) by the challenging group, and (3) by its antagonist, and (4) the challenging group's level of satisfaction with its achievement at the end of the challenge. In many cases, we were unable to get sufficient information on one or more of these perceptions, in which case we coded what we could. The codes covered changes both during the period of the challenge and in the following 15 years.

For each goal, then, it was possible to get a series of pluses, minuses, or zeroes as follows: when a source (historian, challenging group, or antagonist) agreed that at least half of the relevant targets had responded in the desired direction, we recorded a plus (+). Similarly, when the group itself was at least partially satisfied with the outcome, we recorded a plus. A minus (−) was recorded when a source asserted that less than half of the targets responded as desired, and the group was no more satisfied at the end of the challenge than when it began. If there was insufficient information on the perceptions of one or another source, a zero (0) was recorded. Thus, each goal area received a field of four codes (e.g., +++0, −++−, −−−0, etc.).

Most of the groups had multiple goals and, within each goal cluster, multiple aspects of concern. Thus, a group typically had several fields of the sort described above, sometimes as many as a dozen or more. Again, a summary measure is essential to deal with this large set of measures of new advantages.

The summary measure adopted has four categories:

1. *Twenty groups (38 percent) received no new advantages.* These groups had minuses and zeroes on all clusters.

2. *Twenty-six groups (49 percent) received new advantages.* These groups had at least one positive field (i.e., pluses, no more than two zeroes, and no minuses) in a majority of their areas of concern. In other words, on most of their goals, these groups received a positive response on at least one major aspect.

3. *Four groups (7 percent) received peripheral advantages.* These were groups that had some positive fields but did not meet the full definition of a group receiving new advantages.

4. *Three groups (6 percent) received equivocal advantages.* These were groups with mixed fields (some pluses and some minuses concerning the same goal). In other words, these were groups on which disagreement existed among different observers on whether goals had been realized or not.

The seven groups in the last two categories will be combined

FIGURE 3–2
Outcomes for the Sample of Challenging Groups Based on Summary Measures of Acceptance and New Advantages

| | | *Minimal Acceptance Relationship* | |
		Yes	No
New Advantages	Yes	Full response = 20 38%	Preemption = 6 11%
	No (or equivocal and peripheral)	Co-optation = 5 9%	Collapse = 22 42%

$n - 53$

with the no-advantage group for analysis purposes. Figure 3–2 shows the distribution of the 53 groups in the four outcome categories described above. In many analyses, we will examine each summary measure separately as we explore the relative influence of some variable of interest on these different measures of outcome. Henceforth, when I use the term "success," it will refer to either or both outcome measures in those contexts in which there is no need to differentiate between them.

chapter four

The Strategy of Thinking Small

There is a certain absurdity in comparing a group that seeks a modest change and threatens no major redistribution of power with one that seeks to sweep aside the old order and all its supporting institutions. For modesty of aspiration, few challenging groups can compete with the Society for the Promotion of Manual Labor in Literary Institutions. This quaint effort of the 1830s was one of several reform efforts supported by the Tappan brothers. The group's mobilization effort consisted primarily of lectures by its paid general agent, Theodore Weld. No state militias were necessary to hold back the crowds aroused by Weld's impassioned pleas. In fact, Weld, who was apparently a skillful speaker, frequently found it expedient to build his audience by advertising his topic as temperance, then using the occasion to make an additional pitch on educational reform.

Weld invoked an image of the college student and seminarian that 150 years has not seriously dated. His portrait depicted the typical collegian "with his feet elevated upon a mantelpiece as high as his head, body bent like a halfmoon or a horseshoe, lolling, stretching, yawning, smoking, snoring." Strong physical labor was recommended for this shiftless lot, to "tone the body, stimulate the intellect, safeguard the student's morals by occupying his spare time, teach him useful skills, promote industry, originality, and manliness. By cheapening the cost of education, it would broaden the country's intellectual base, and by demonstrating the compatibility of physical and intellectual endeavor, it would do away with absurd social distinctions between those who work with their brains and those who produce with their hands" (Thomas, 1950).

In contrast, although in a way equally quaint, consider the Communist Labor Party. This was the name taken by the so-called Benjamin Gitlow-John Reed, left-wing faction of the Socialist Party when they broke away in the summer of 1919. It was a period of considerable hysteria, stimulated by the success of the Bolshevik revolution and the substantial labor unrest in the United States. Nineteen nineteen was the year of the Seattle general strike, the Lawrence textile strike, the Boston police strike, the national coal strike and a large steel strike involving 365,000 workers.

The fledgling and ineffectual Communist Labor Party was a natural target of the various organs of the antired hysteria. First, in November, 1919, many of its members, including Gitlow, were arrested in raids growing out of the New York State Senate's Lusk Committee and its investigations of "seditious activity." There was considerable competition among anticommunist entrepreneurs of the day; group members were also arrested in large numbers in raids initiated by the District Attorney of Chicago and U.S. Attorney General Mitchell Palmer. Gitlow also reports a great deal of additional harassment (Gitlow, 1940), and he personally was sentenced and jailed for more than a year. John Reed once faced three indictments at the same time. Most of the leaders "lived in a half-world of indictments, trials, defense committees, convictions, sentences, and appeals" (Draper, 1957).

What were the goals of this beleaguered group? "The Communist Labor Party of America declares itself in complete accord with the principles of Communism as laid down in the Manifesto of the Third International formed at Moscow."[1] This included the organization and training of the working class for the capture of state power and the establishment of new, working class, government machinery. The new working class government would "transfer

---

[1] From the "Party and Labor Program," reprinted in the *Report of the Joint Legislative Committee Investigating Seditious Activities*, (Lusk Committee), April 24, 1920, Senate of the State of New York.

private property in the means of production and distribution to the working class government, to be administered by the workers themselves. It shall nationalize the great trusts and financial institutions. It shall abolish capitalist agricultural production" (ibid). In short, their aim was a classical revolutionary set of goals.

The revelation that the Communist Labor Party was unsuccessful will come as a surprise to no one. Organizationally, it gave up its existence in less than a year, uniting with the Ruthenberg faction of the Communist Party to form the United Communist Party. Both groups were heavily depleted by the devastating and effective arrests and deportations to which their members were subjected. The United Communist Party, in turn, went through several more fusions and fissions with no noticeable positive response on any outcome measure.

The Society for the Promotion of Manual Labor in Literary Institutions had the more complicated fate of preemption but did not live much longer as an organization. By 1833, Arthur and Lewis Tappan and Theodore Weld were becoming interested in other causes, especially abolitionism. With Weld's resignation to pursue a career in the ministry, the Society essentially ceased to function. During its existence, the manual labor system was adopted in some form by many colleges, theological seminaries, several medical schools, and several hundred academies. Many of the changes were short-lived, however, and, with no one pressing the challenge, "the system declined nearly as rapidly as it arose and had been abandoned by most institutions before 1840" (Anderson, 1913).

What meaning can there be in comparing the fate of groups as different as the Society for the Promotion of Manual Labor in Literary Institutions and the Communist Labor Party? Very little, if we are able to discover nothing more than the half-truth that the less one tries to get, the more likely he is to get it. Clearly, many groups have incommensurate tasks. The challenge is to discover two things about the goals these groups have undertaken:

1. Is differential success related to aspects of group goals that are less obvious than the magnitude of the group's ambition?

2. When we compare groups with more or less commensurate tasks, do we still find major differences in their rate of success?

The second of these questions is really the concern of later chapters. We will need to constantly reassure ourselves that any apparent difference in outcome due to strategies of mobilization, influence, or internal organization are not due simply to differences in underlying goals[2] or type of group. The remainder of this chapter explores the first question. We will examine the "think small" formula for success in more detail to see how well it fits the 53 groups here.

THREE CHOICES

Roberta Ash (1972), like a number of other observers before her, notes the failure of radical movements in America which have "functioned mainly to impress elites with the relative mildness of reform movement demands." Although not intended as a reproach to radical groups with which she has much sympathy, her interpretation of the past supports the "think small" formula for success. "The broader the goals of a social movement, the more central its focus, and the greater its threat to class structure," she writes, "the less likely it will be to succeed" (Ash, p. 12).

Magnitude of goals is a multidimensional concept, and Ash is helpful in suggesting three aspects. "All movements must make a series of choices:

Between single issue demands and multiple demands.

Between radical demands and demands that do not attack the legitimacy of present distributions of wealth and power.

Between influencing elites (or even incorporating movement members into the elite) and attempting to replace elites" (Ash, p. 230).

DISPLACING THE ANTAGONIST

Some 30 percent (16) of the 53 challenging groups had goals requiring the removal of at least some of their antagonists. It is misleading, however, if this conjures up the guillotine. Although sev-

---

[2] It is useful to think of a goal as an *internal justification* for collective action planned by the group. It is internal in the sense that it is considered a justification by group members themselves and is not simply trotted out on public occasions to impress outsiders. It is a justification in the sense that X is a goal if group members agree that the statement "Action A will lead to X" is *if true* a positive reason for doing A. They may, of course, think that Action A will not really lead to X but this does not affect the status of X as a desirable end-state. Since a group can have multiple goals, a member might argue that A will lead to X but will detract from Y and Z. If this is generally accepted by members as a valid argument against A, if true, this implies that Y and Z are also goals of the group.

Among goals defined in this way, there are two types: external goals and organizational goals. The latter refer to the enhancement of the strength and ability of the challenging group rather than to the realization of new advantages for the group's beneficiary. The discussion here focuses on external goals.

eral fully expected to use force to overcome resistance, most wanted less to destroy antagonists than to retire them to peaceful pastures.

Only half of these groups were left-wing, and some of these were nonviolent in both ideology and practice. The Brotherhood of the Cooperative Commonwealth, for example, hoped to displace the government of the state of Washington by means of a rather implausible colonization scheme (see pp. 3–5). Socialists, migrating to Washington and establishing colonies there, would achieve political power through constitutional means, "call a constitutional convention, inaugurate public ownership of all the means of production and distribution, and solve the money question through use of labor exchanges. . . . Other states would be inspired by the success of the first, and soon the entire nation would be socialist" (Kipnis, 1968).

Likewise, the eight nonsocialist groups did not necessarily foresee bloody battles in replacing their antagonist. While the Christian Front against Communism was not averse to extralegal means, the American Party of the 1880s was a straightforward electoral challenger. Of the 16 groups that hoped to displace their antagonist, only six made no actual use of the electoral system in their influence attempts, and even some of these accepted some role for it in theory.

How successful are the groups that aim to displace one or more antagonist compared to the 70 percent that merely wanted to change its policies or organization in some way? Note that acceptance here must mean one of two things, either self-acceptance or acceptance by an antagonist other than the one being potentially displaced. Self-acceptance means some degree of successful displacement—for example, winning offices by a third party.

Figure 4–1 indicates a dismal success rate by either criteria. Two of the groups (12 percent) achieved some minimal acceptance, but only one, the League of Deliverance, achieved new advantages as well. The Bull Moose Party (Progressive Party) failed to elect Theodore Roosevelt president but had some success in congressional and state elections, most notably in electing Hiram Johnson and Robert LaFollette. As for new advantages, we quote from Amos Pinchot, one of the party's major protagonists:

> The party had an aspiration instead of an issue, a most creditable aspiration, but one for whose accomplishment its platform provided no

understandable means. Social and industrial justice! The square deal! Destruction of invisible government! The dawn of a new day! But how realize these ends? The answer of the Progressives was, "Make Roosevelt president." And when it became clear that they could not do that, the Progressives disbanded and the country knew them no more (Pinchot, 1958).

The League of Deliverance won both acceptance and new advantages, but there is some reason to question whether displacement of its antagonist was a true goal. This nativist group of the 1880s tried to prevent the employment of Chinese labor by boycotting those businesses that continued to employ Chinese. "Don't patronize Grass or Butterfield; they sell Chinese-made boots and shoes. Avoid them! They are traitors to their race," said one of the League's leaflets. However, destruction of such businesses was really more means than goal—that is, not a justification in its own right. By getting rid of its Chinese workers, a business could buy peace with the League and many did just that. Ira Cross (1935)

FIGURE 4–1
Success Rate by Displacement of Antagonists

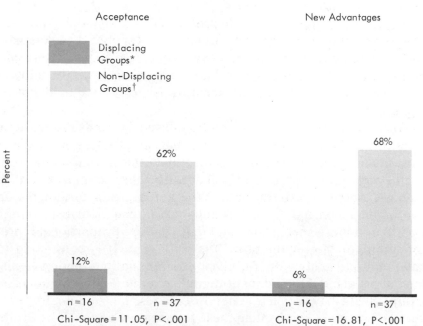

* Groups that hoped to displace one or more antagonists.
† Groups that hoped only to change the policies or organization of antagonists.

describes how "one factory which had from 500 to 600 Chinese on its payroll replaced them with white workers, as did many other employers."

With the possible exception above, then, no group that attempted to displace its antagonist, even by peaceful means, was successful in winning new advantages. In contrast, two-thirds of the remaining groups achieved this success.

MULTIPLE-ISSUE GROUPS

There is a fundamental ambiguity in the concept of "issue" that makes it difficult to address the question of whether groups with multiple-issue demands are more or less successful than those with a single demand. Is abolishing capitalism a single- or multiple-issue demand? Is a group that wants to both raise wages and better working conditions for a group of laborers making a single-issue demand or two separate ones? It is not difficult to formulate any group's demands as either single or multiple. If a group has several issues, the level of generality can be raised so that they are seen as aspects of a single, larger issue, or any larger issue can be subdivided into different aspects.

Ideologies group issues differently. A Marxist does not see American intervention in the Dominican Republic and Vietnam and the neglect of domestic poverty as separate issues but as part of a single, larger issue. A non-Marxist participant in the antiwar movement might see these as separate issues that should not be aggregated.

To ask whether a group has multiple-issue demands is to assume a clarity in the unit one is counting that simply does not exist. I have made several attempts to reformulate this question in a more useful way, but even the one I will describe here contains a considerable element of arbitrariness. Whether a group formulates an overarching demand (e.g., "establish National Socialism in the U.S.") or a more specific demand (e.g., "adopt proportional representation" or "lower the tariff") is irrelevant. It is considered to have multiple goals only if it gives programmatic attention to distinct subgoals in different institutional spheres. Thus, two socialist groups might have similar general demands, but one might never get to the point of subdividing these for separate action. The Brotherhood of the Cooperative Commonwealth and the Communist Labor Party, described above, are both considered "single-issue" groups under this definition. One focused its energy on a single program, colonization, and the other was so busy with constant defense that it scarcely had the luxury of initiating any action program, let alone several.

The National Student League, on the other hand, was equally Marxist in orientation but adopted a number of specific causes as its own. It had a series of campus-oriented concerns such as ending compulsory ROTC and compulsory chapel and gaining equal educational opportunities for women and blacks. It cooperated with other groups in the early 1930s in sponsoring antiwar strikes and involved itself in the bitter struggle of the coal miners in Harlan County, Kentucky. No doubt, many National Student League participants saw these separate struggles as part of the process of building "consciousness" for the larger struggle, but they became goals in their own right as well. Since they involved different antagonists in different institutional spheres, we classify such a group as having multiple issues.

About one-sixth of the groups (9) have multiple-issue demands in the above sense. Five of these are political parties, making an appeal to the electorate on different issues. These five, incidentally, include all of the pure third parties, pure in the sense that they were created to contest elections. They vary in political orientation with two nativist, two reform, and one socialist group among their number.

There are two reasons why we might expect a greater degree of success for these multi-issue groups. First, only a group that has managed to survive for a little while can be expected to begin the process of differentiating action programs in different areas. The very idea of multiple issues seems to imply some strength and stability. Second, with many hooks in the water, it seems that one would be more likely to catch a fish or two.

Figure 4-2 indicates no support for these expectations. A couple of the groups manage to achieve a minimal acceptance relationship, but none win new advantages. The Bull Moose Party is one of the exceptions on the basis of a few electoral victories below the level of the Presidency. The other exception, the American Student Union, was a "popular front" group of the middle and late 1930s. It grew from a merger between the socialist-dominated Student League for Industrial Democracy and the communist-dominated National Student League, described above. During its convention in 1938, the delegates received a letter of greetings from President

FIGURE 4–2
Success Rate by Multi-Issue Demands

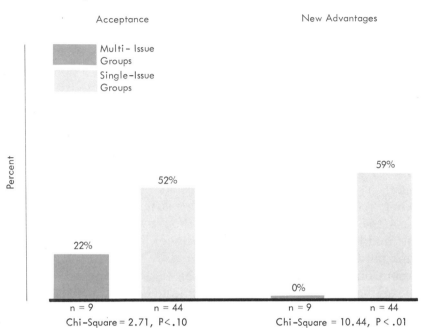

Roosevelt, as well as messages from the mayor of New York, the president of CCNY, and the women's director of the Democratic National Committee. As one former member and critic writes, "The student movement was now completely respectable, completely pro-administration, and completely emasculated" (Hal Draper in Simon, 1967). For even this group, however, co-optation rather than full response was its fate. Despite the many hooks these multi-issue groups had in the water, the fish apparently weren't biting.

RADICAL GOALS

If the idea of multiple issues presented us with problems of ambiguity, the idea of radical demands is even more formidable. There are, of course, some clear cases. No one would have any difficulty classifying the Communist Labor Party and the Society for the Promotion of Manual Labor in Literary Institutions. Assume that we mean by "radical," the degree of threat to existing distributions of wealth and power. In judging a group, we immediately confront a danger of tautology. It is tempting to judge threat by the response of the threatened. If an antagonist reacts with rage and horror, marshalling all his forces in defense, we would appear to be dealing with a severe threat. If he ignores the challenger or responds benignly, the threat presumably cannot be too great. But these responses of the antagonist are essential parts of our outcome measures, and to use them also to measure radicalness involves us in circularity. If a radical group is defined as one that is fiercely and stubbornly resisted, then, in examining success, we can only find that radical groups are fiercely and stubbornly resisted. The problem becomes one of defining radicalness of goals independently of response.

Common sense language here is a source of considerable confusion. Groups that were once called "radical" are now seen as mild and accommodating. Was the Federal Suffrage Association radical? It was certainly considered so by many, and one could easily argue that it challenged "the legitimacy of present distributions of wealth and power." But, today, few would claim that it fundamentally altered the position of women in society. Not long ago, the setting of wages and working conditions and the right to hire and fire workers were seen as fundamental and exclusive management prerogatives; the demand that such prerogatives be shared with worker representatives was highly threatening to many employers and their allies. With a handful of exceptions, all of our groups appeared to their antagonists to be making radical demands.

If the term "radical" is hopelessly unclear, perhaps we can gain a purchase on this question by a more oblique approach. We coded a number of specific questions about the concerns of the challenging group. Specifically, we asked whether in its influence attempts, the group was concerned with (1) altering the scope of authority of all or some of its antagonists, (2) altering the procedures used by these antagonists, (3) altering the personnel of its antagonists, and/or (4) destroying or replacing all or some of its antagonists. If the answer to these four questions for a group is uniformly negative, we can call its goals "limited"; they are concerned simply with changing the content of some specific policy. If the answer to any one of these questions is positive, we will call its goals "more-than-limited."

More-than-limited is somewhat less than what many would mean by radical, but presumably it includes, among others, what most people mean by the term. It includes the Communist Labor Party and the Anarcho-Communists, but it also includes many unions, engaged in challenges to management authority and hiring procedures. It includes the Federal Suffrage Association and the American Proportional Representation League, both bent on altering electoral procedures. It includes, in fact, about two-thirds of the sample.

By definition, none of the 18 groups with limited goals include the replacement of the antagonist as part of their objective. We already know that groups which aim to displace their target do poorly. Thus, we need to make sure that differences between those with limited and those with more-than-limited goals are not due simply to the presence among the latter of a good many groups that aim to displace their target. In Figure 4–3, we subdivide those with more-than-limited goals to distinguish the displacing groups from the rest.

It is apparent that having limited or more-than-limited goals

FIGURE 4–3
Success Rate by Limited Goals

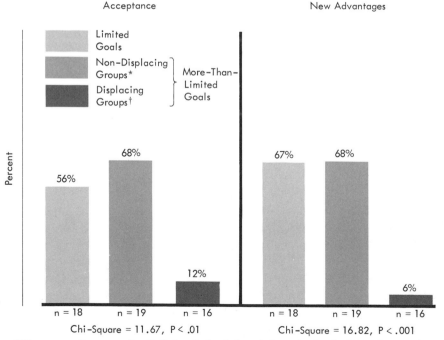

* These groups have more-than-limited goals, but their goals do not involve the destruction or replacement of antagonists.

† These groups have more-than-limited goals *including* the destruction or replacement of antagonists.

makes no difference in its own right. Once we remove the displacing groups with their low rate of success, the success rate for the others is indistinguishable. While about two-thirds of the groups with limited goals achieve new advantages, about two-thirds of the others do also as long as they do not try to replace or destroy their antagonist as well.

THINKING SMALL REEVALUATED

It appears that there is some modest advantage in setting one's sights low. There are 18 groups with the combination of limited goals, a single-issue area, and no displacement of antagonists; two-thirds of them gain new advantages and 56 percent gain some minimal acceptance.

But lack of ambition is neither necessary nor sufficient for success. Even groups with modest aims often fail. Furthermore, we can identify more precisely what it is about the goals of the more ambitious groups that is most closely associated with failure.

First, having limited goals makes little difference in the fate of a group as long as those with more-than-limited goals do not try to displace their antagonist. Second, while groups with multiple-issue demands do poorly, it turns out that eight of the nine also are attempting to displace their antagonist. The one exception here is the American Student Union, which may account for its partial success on the criterion of acceptance. Thus, there is no clear evidence for an *independent* effect of multiple-issue demands on the fate of these groups; their low success rate may be due simply to the fact that they also aim to displace their antagonist. On the other hand, there are eight single-issue groups that have displacement as an objective, and with the exception of the League of Deliverance (the anti-Chinese group discussed above, pp. 43–44) they are uniformly unsuccessful in spite of their more concentrated focus.

It appears then, perhaps not too surprisingly, that what really stands in the way of success for the ambitious challenger is not diffuse objectives but targets of change who are unwilling to cooperate in their own demise. It is not that these antagonists would rather fight than yield half-a-loaf but rather that no half-loaf exists that will give these particular challenging groups what they seek. The antagonist must resist or give up the ghost. An antagonist begins with resources while the challenging group usually starts from scratch. Thus, it is not surprising that a challenging group attempting to displace it has a bad time of it, regardless of the means employed or the narrowness or broadness of its goals.

A NOTE ON GROUP SIZE

We know now what it is about group goals that we must consider in interpreting subsequent results. Should we also be concerned about group size? Although it is not theoretically interesting in its own right, if size has an important influence on success, we will need to control its effects in interpreting other relationships.

Group size is a very crude variable for two reasons. First, there are great differences among groups in the definition of membership. For many groups, the line between supporter and member is not sharp, and "membership" is more psychological than formal. To be a member of the Bull Moose Party involved no more than psychological identification; in contrast, the Communist Labor Party required a formal application, including a pledge renouncing membership in any other party, and each application was approved or disapproved at a formal meeting. The Tobacco Night Riders required a blood oath of new members. However, more than one-fourth of the groups (15) did not even maintain an official membership list.

Second, it is not uncommon for groups to inflate membership claims to impress outsiders. Father Coughlin, for example, claimed over seven-and-a-half million members for his National Union for Social Justice, but some outside observers were willing to grant only that the group had well over a million members at its height. When such discrepancies occurred, the more conservative figure was used here, usually that of an outside observer.

The measure of size, then, is a gross one, the estimated peak membership during the period of challenge. The 53 groups vary from under 1,000 to many millions and are divided here into classes differing by orders of magnitude (i.e., 10^3, 10^4, 10^5, 10^6). About half the groups had less than 10,000 "members" at their peak and about half had more.

Do groups that think small grow big? The answer is, not any more so than others. The 16 displacing groups are well-distributed over the size categories — three are under 1,000, four are over 100,000 and the rest are in between. The same lack of relationship holds for groups with multiple-issue demands.

One might expect that larger groups would be more successful in general. First, larger groups should have larger amounts of resources at their disposal. Numbers, one might think, mean power for a challenging group. Second, size might be a symptom as well as a cause of success. A group in the process of succeeding ought to find it easier to get partisans than would an apparent lost cause.[3]

The relationship between size and success is somewhat complex, as Figures 4–4 and 4–5 indicate. There is only a negligible difference between groups of different size in gaining new advantages. Larger groups are not much more likely to achieve the changes they desire than smaller ones. There is, however, a more substantial difference in gaining acceptance. Here, bigness seems to help; only 30 percent of the groups with under 10,000 members win some minimal acceptance, while almost two-thirds of those over 10,000 are successful on this measure.

That size has a different relationship to acceptance than it does to new advantages indicates that there is something interesting here concerning co-opted and preempted groups. Preempted groups tend to be small — only one of six is over 10,000; co-opted groups tend to be large — only one of five is under 10,000.

What conclusions can we draw about size? Overall, it is essentially irrelevant with respect to a group's gaining new advantages. However, there is a complex interaction between size and gaining acceptance which we can see in Figure 4–6. Among those groups that gain new advantages, if they are over 10,000, they are almost certain to gain acceptance as well; only one in 14 fails to achieve this additional form of success. Of those under 10,000, only 58 percent achieve both measures of success. Among those groups that fail to gain new advantages, large size is a help in at least gaining some minimal acceptance. For those under 10,000 only one in 15 gains some minimal acceptance while one-third of the larger groups gain at least this form of success.

Preemption serves as an incomplete form of full response. Among the groups that achieved new advantages, some grew large and gained acceptance as well; some remained small and a substantial minority of these never achieved acceptance. Perhaps their success came too easily and early. It is worth noting that five of the six preempted groups gained new advantages within the first five years of their challenge. In a few cases, there seemed to be no par-

---

[3] This argument, as we will see in the next chapter, is based on premises that are called into question by the "theory of public goods."

FIGURE 4-4
Acceptance by Size of Group

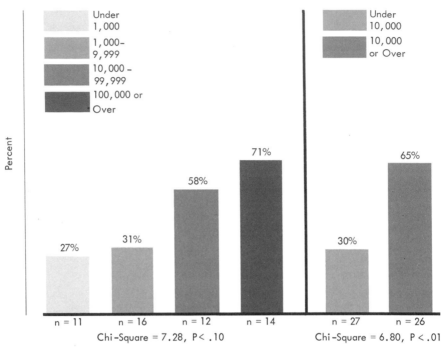

Chi-Square = 7.28, P< .10   Chi-Square = 6.80, P< .01

FIGURE 4-5
New Advantages by Size of Group

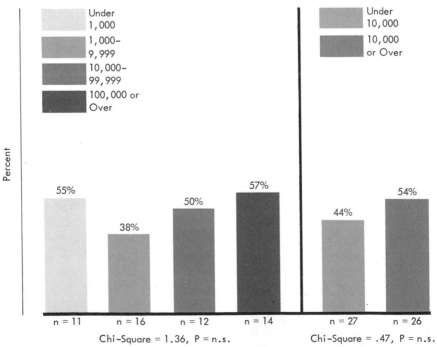

Chi-Square = 1.36, P = n.s.   Chi-Square = .47, P = n.s.

FIGURE 4–6
Acceptance and Size Controlling for New Advantages

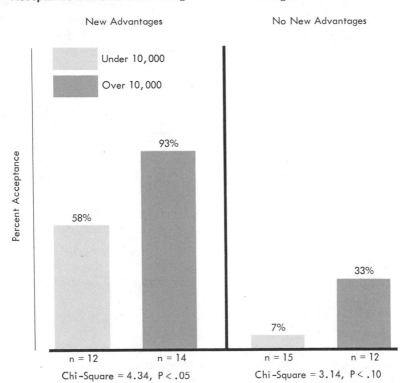

ticular desire for acceptance, once gains had been achieved. The Tobacco Night Riders, for example, were a clandestine group and never anticipated or sought acceptance for themselves. But they were allied with the Planter's Protective Association, and this partner came to control 90 percent of the tobacco market and was dealt with by all of the major tobacco companies. In some other cases — for example, the Society for the Promotion of Manual Labor in Literary Institutions — partial success seemed to spoil the appetite, as key activists turned to other issues. In any event, a certain number of groups won new advantages but never became sufficiently established and formidable to win acceptance. Such groups tended to be relatively small.

Co-optation, by a similar argument, is an alternative to collapse. A group that not only failed to achieve new advantages, but failed to grow as well, ended up collapsing without acceptance. But others got large and some, developing a stake in the maintenance of the organization, made their peace with their antagonists at the expense of their supposed beneficiaries. Thus, a certain number of groups never won new advantages but became sufficiently established and formidable to win acceptance. Such groups tended to be relatively large.

REFERENCES

Anderson, L.F. "The Manual Labor School Movement" *Educational Review* 46 (1913).

Ash, Roberta. *Social Movements in America*. Chicago: Markham, 1972.

Cross, Ira B. *A History of the Labor Movement in California*. Berkeley: University of California, 1935.

Draper, Hal. "The Student Movement of the Thirties." Rita Simon (ed.), *As We Saw the Thirties*. Urbana: University of Illinois Press, 1967.

Draper, Theodore. *The Roots of American Communism*. New York: Viking Press, 1957.

Gitlow, Benjamin. *I Confess: The Truth about American Communism*. New York: E.P. Dutton, 1940.

Kipnis, Ira. *The American Socialist Movement, 1887–1912*. New York: Greenwood Press, 1968.

Pinchot, Amos. *History of the Progressive Party, 1912–1916*. New York: New York University Press, 1958.

Thomas, Benjamin P. *Theodore Weld: Crusader for Freedom*. New Brunswick: Rutgers University Press, 1950.

chapter five

The Limits of Solidarity

"It is often taken for granted," Mancur Olson writes, ". . . that groups of individuals with common interests usually attempt to further those common interests. Groups of individuals with common interests are expected to act on behalf of their common interests much as single individuals are often expected to act on behalf of their personal interests" (1965, p. 1).

In his seminal work, *The Logic of Collective Action,* Olson calls this underlying assumption into question with highly provocative results. "It does *not* follow, because all of the individuals in a group would gain if they achieved their group objective, that they would act to achieve that objective, even if they were all rational and self-interested." Indeed, except under certain special conditions, "rational, self-interested individuals will not act to achieve their common or group interests" (p. 2).

This apparent paradox arises from the nature of the common interests that are pursued through collective action.

> The basic and most elementary goods or services provided by government, like defense and police protection, . . . are such that they go to everyone or practically everyone in the nation. It would obviously not be feasible, if indeed it were possible, to deny the protection provided by the military services, the police, and the courts to those who did not voluntarily pay their share of the costs of govern-

ment, and taxation is accordingly necessary. The common or collective benefits provided by governments are usually called "public goods" by economists. . . . A common, collective or public good is here defined as any good such that, if any person X_i in a group $X_l, \ldots X_i, \ldots X_n$ consumes it, it cannot feasibly be withheld from the others in that group" (Olson, p. 14).[1]

It is important to note that a collective good is defined for a particular group. A given social change, for example, may affect only some people and leave the lot of others unchanged. Assuming that if produced, all members of the first group will be affected, it is a collective good for them. If it is also feasible to supply the benefits to others on an individual basis, it is a private good for these others. Olson illustrates this point with the example of a parade to which one can buy tickets. It is a private good for those who must purchase seats but a public good for those who live in houses overlooking the parade route.

The word "feasible" in Olson's definition should be understood broadly. Even if it is technically feasible to supply the goods privately, the definition holds if it is impractical or inconvenient to do so. In the example above, a high wall might be erected to block the view of those who did not purchase tickets, but the economic and political costs of such action would undoubtedly make it impractical.

The changes sought by challenging groups are collective goods for those who are affected by such changes. This is true whether they approve of the group's program or not, for, as Albert Hirschman (1970) puts it, "He who says public goods says public evils. . . . What is a public good for some — say, a plentiful supply of police dogs and atomic bombs — may well be judged a public evil by others in the same community" (p. 101). The distinguishing characteristic of collective goods, then, is that one receives the "benefits," dubious or real, whether one has paid for them and wants them or not.

Now if we suppose a group large enough that the contribution or efforts of any one member would not make a difference in

---

[1] This definition emphasizes a property of collective goods called "nonexclusiveness." There is a second property, called "nonrivalness of supply," meaning that the consumption by one member of the group does not reduce the supply available to others. The social changes sought by challenging groups are "pure" public goods, meeting both properties, and we will not need to distinguish between the properties here.

whether the group achieves its goals, why should a given member contribute? If he is not conscious of the value of the goals sought, clearly he will have no motive to contribute, but, even if he values their achievement a great deal, he still will have no self-interested reason to help. It is against his individual interests to pay any costs since *he will enjoy the benefits produced by the group whether or not he has helped to support it.* He will be individually better off pursuing his personal interests and taking an effortless, free ride while others make sacrifices for his group interests.

Olson applies his analysis to Marxian class theory, arguing that the critics of Marx are wrong in thinking that he overestimated rationality in expecting people to pursue their class interest. On the contrary, Olson argues, Marx underestimated it "for class-oriented action will not occur if the individuals that make up a class act rationally. If a person is in the bourgeois class, he may well want a government that represents his class. But it does not follow that it will be in his interest to work to see that such a government comes to power. If there is such a government, he will benefit from its policies, whether or not he has supported it, for by Marx's own hypothesis, it will work for his class interests." It follows that the rational thing for an individual bourgeois to do "is to ignore his *class* interests and to spend his energies on his *personal* interests" (Olson, pp. 105–6).

It cannot be taken for granted, then, that individuals will tend to organize to pursue their collective interests. On the contrary, they will not, except under special conditions that will be examined in detail below. I accept the basic premise – that when individuals sometimes unite to pursue their collective interest, this requires an explanation. It cannot be taken for granted as something "natural."

Although Olson does not use the term, the groups face a problem of internal social control. There are three basic ways of handling such a problem: through constraints, inducements, or persuasion. Constraints and inducements involve the use of negative and positive sanctions, respectively (cf. Gamson, 1968). Persuasion works on the orientation of the actor rather than his situation.

> There is an interesting variety of words used to describe this social control technique – some of them highly pejorative and others complimentary. The approving words include education, persuasion, therapy, rehabilitation, and, perhaps more neutrally, socialization. The disapproving words include indoctrination, manipulation, prop-

aganda and "brainwashing." The choice of words is merely a reflection of the speaker's attitude toward [the group doing the controlling] (Gamson, p. 125).

There is in Olson's argument a strong bias or skepticism about the effectiveness of "internalized" social control or persuasion. Olson can see readily enough how a group can induce members to join by means of selective, private rewards given only to those who participate. Similarly, he can understand readily enough that members can be constrained to join by threat of personal harm for not participating. But he really does not view group loyalty or solidarity as a meaningful form of control. He grants the usefulness of "social incentives." The social approval that comes from participating or the ostracism that comes from remaining aloof may be quite important in mobilizing individuals. But these remain social *sanctions,* rewards and punishments analogous to material sanctions, and not a form of persuasion.

Clearly, it is possible to argue for the effectiveness of normative appeals as well. James Coleman (1973), for example, addresses the general problem of why individuals are willing to surrender so much freedom to corporate actors. He recognizes selective incentives as part of the process. "When a person joins a guild, union, or professional association, he yields control over certain actions (as well as monetary fees) expecting to gain thereby." But there are more subtle examples as well involving "those corporate actors which persons invest in and sacrifice for with no tangible returns. These range from the sports team in an elementary school, to the nation for which men may give their lives. Such investments pay intangible but directly experienced rewards in the sense of pleasure a person experiences in being on a winning team or the sense of . . . well-being he experiences when his nation does well."

The psychological processes involved in this pleasure are centered on identification and the investment of part of oneself in collective actors. To reap the rewards of such identification requires commitment. The greater the sacrifice and effort involved, the greater is the investment of self, and, hence, the greater the personal satisfaction (or disappointment) with the achievements of the collective actor. Note that there is no contradiction of Olson's basic premise here, since I refer to a form of private personal satisfaction over and above any collective benefits produced by the group. In this sense, it is still a kind of selective incentive, but not one that is mediated by the group as a sanction. It is not useful to treat it as simply another form of inducement in the same category as a private good or service that the group provides to its members. Rather, it is an alternative, internalized means of overcoming the free-rider problem.

Olson makes some effort to address the point above. He grants that "the theory developed here is . . . not very useful for the analysis of groups that are characterized by a low degree of rationality, in the sense in which that word is used here. Take for example the occasional band of committed people who continue to work through their organizaitons for admittedly lost causes. Such a labor of love is not rational, at least from the economic perspective, for it is pointless to make sacrifices which by definition will be ineffective" (Olson, p. 161).

But why speak of "lost causes"? By Olson's own argument, the statement should apply as well to the occasional band of committed people who make sacrifices for causes that have some chance of success. He notes Lenin's insight in *What Is to Be Done?* (Lenin, 1929) for the "need to rely on a committed, self-sacrificing, and disciplined minority rather than on the common interests of the mass of the proletariat." Some members of the vanguard might be motivated by the personal benefits of their organizational position should the challenge succeed; it would make sense for them to invest energy for an essentially personal benefit. But commitment and self-sacrifice imply a willingness to continue when a cost-benefit analysis yields a negative expected value. One doesn't speak of self-sacrifice when personal interest dictates support. For most challenging groups, the vanguard is distinguished by its larger risks and investments in pursuit of little more than the promise of achieving collective goods. They are as irrational in Olson's terms as the pursuers of a lost cause.

Implicit in Olson's argument, then, is a belief in the insufficiency of ideological appeals except for a special category of "mass movements" about which he purports to say little. However, many of the groups he uses to illustrate his argument do make heavy use of appeals to solidarity. "Oh, you can't scare me, I'm sticking to the Union" says one of the many songs of the labor movement in its period of challenge. Many groups seek an enlarged notion of self — an identification of self and group interest such that an individual experiences personal pleasure from the achievement of a collective good.

There can be little doubt that such "irrational" loyalty is highly functional for a group, and, in fact, it may be absolutely vital. If it is too much to ask of members in general, at least it is necessary for a core of dedicated activists to have it. Although Olson gives little importance to loyalty, we turn to another political economist, Albert Hirschman (1970), for an argument in which loyalty plays a central role.

Hirschman is addressing a somewhat different problem — the conditions under which dissatisfied members of an organization will choose to leave or to stay and attempt to change it. Loyalty, he argues, "is at its most functional when it looks most irrational, when loyalty means strong attachments to an organization that does not seem to warrant such attachment because it is so much like another one that is also available. Such seemingly irrational loyalties are often encountered, for example, in relation to clubs, football teams, and political parties." Why is such loyalty so important? Because, "it can neutralize within certain limits the tendency of the most quality-conscious . . . members to be the first to exit. . . . Thus, loyalty, far from being irrational, can serve the socially useful purpose of preventing deterioration from becoming cumulative, as it so often does when there is no barrier to exit" (Hirschman, pp. 79 and 81).

It is not difficult to extend this argument to challenging groups. It is especially in large groups where one individual can hardly hope by his sacrifices to make a real difference in the group's achieving its goals that loyalty is needed. Terms like "irrational" obscure the issue. This loyalty remains "irrational" in the individual sense in which Olson uses it, even while it is functional and even necessary for the group to succeed. But an individual, imbued with a sense of responsibility to the group, might recognize the necessity of personal sacrifice, not in spite of, but *because of* the full force of Olson's argument. And he may appeal to others on this basis rather than on the basis of personal interest. "Ask not what your challenging group can do for you but what you can do for it," he might intone.

The thrust of this discussion is that Olson's argument must be evaluated in empirical terms. It does not follow *logically* from the theory of collective goods that loyalty or solidarity will be insufficient as a means of social control. What does follow logically is only that, to be successful, groups must find *some* way of overcoming the free-rider problem. It is Olson's hypothesis that, because of the overwhelming claim of personal interests, appeals to solidarity will not do the job adequately. Granted that it may be sufficient for some few committed loyalists, a group that asks voluntary sacrifices from all its members will not succeed. Stating the issues in these terms, we can examine the sufficiency of this form of social control for the 53 challenging groups studied here.

UNIVERSALISTIC GROUPS

Olson attempts to state some of the limits of his argument. While the theory is not limited to situations where only monetary or material interests are at stake, "it is true that this theory, like any other theory, is less helpful in some cases than in others. . . . The theory is not at all sufficient where philanthropic lobbies, that is, lobbies that voice concern about some group other than the group that supports the lobby, or religious lobbies, are concerned. In philanthropic and religious lobbies, the relationships between the purposes and interests of the individual member, and the purposes and interests of the organization, may be so rich and obscure that a theory of the sort developed here cannot provide much insight" (Olson, pp. 159–60).

This is a particularly unfortunate form of special pleading because one of the strengths of Olson's argument is the central insight it gives about these groups. It suggests that they are, in fact, *no different* than supposedly self-interested groups because self-interested groups face an identical problem — how to get members to work for something that they will receive or not receive independently of their individual efforts. In this sense, *all* large groups are "philanthropic," in that support cannot be explained by personal interest.

For Olson to make the distinction is faint-hearted, given the implications of his own argument. For the older group theorists whom he criticizes, the distinction is relevant. They see it as entirely reasonable that individuals with common interests usually attempt to further their common interests while it requires an explanation that individuals should attempt to further someone else's interest or the interests of everybody. But in rejecting the "naturalness" of pursuing one's common interests, Olson shows the distinction to be irrelevant. It is no more in one's personal interest to make sacrifices to achieve the goal of his *particular* group than it is for him to make sacrifices to achieve the good of the whole world

FIGURE 5-1
Success Rate by Universalistic Goals

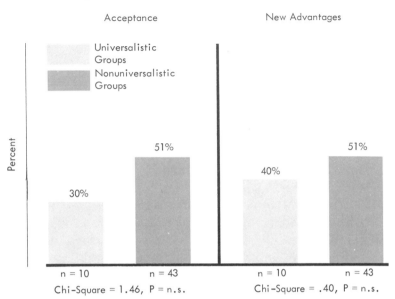

or of some disadvantaged group to which he does not belong. All require an explanation.

Ten of our 53 groups fit what Olson means by "philanthropic" groups, although I find myself very uncomfortable applying this term to the likes of the German-American Bund. I will use, instead, the term *universalistic*. Universalistic groups are defined by a special relationship between their constituency and their beneficiary (see Chapter Two, pp. 15–16). For most of our groups, the constituency is either exclusively or especially affected by the changes that the group seeks. Thus, the major beneficiary and the constituency are identical. For universalistic groups, this is not true. Either everyone will be affected by the changes, the constituency no more or less than others, or some group other than the constituency—for example, some group seen as the victim of special injustice—will benefit more than the constituency. In either case, the major beneficiary and the constituency are not identical, the defining characteristic of universalistic groups.

In Olson's argument, there is no logical reason why universalistic groups should have more difficulty in succeeding than others. Both types must overcome the free-rider problem. Both may need to make use of selective incentives. And if one must appeal to personal loyalty and demand sacrifices, it does not follow that appeals to subgroup loyalties are more effective than universalistic appeals to nation, brotherhood, or social justice. If, in fact, narrower appeals turn out to be more effective, the explanation lies outside of Olson's theory.

The ten universalistic groups in the sample include three abolitionist groups, two right-wing groups, two peace groups, two reform groups, and a religious group that was part of the social gospel movement. Figure 5–1 indicates a slight but insignificant tendency for these groups to be less successful. The three abolitionist groups and the two right-wing groups were unsuccessful for reasons that seem to have little to do with the universalistic nature of their goals. Most of the others achieved some sort of success. It is hard to draw conclusions with confidence on the basis of so few cases, but, in line with Olson's theory, there is no real reason to see the distinction between universalistic and nonuniversalistic groups as an important one in understanding success.

PRIVILEGED GROUPS

Olson's argument applies with full force only to large groups, groups in which one member's contribution will not significantly affect the achievement of the collective goal. Certain smaller groups may be what Olson calls "privileged" groups: "A group such that each of its members, or at least some one of them, has an incentive to see that the collective good is provided, even if he has to bear the full burden of providing it himself" (p. 50). It will not necessarily be provided in the optimal amount, but the general argument against personal interest does not apply where the benefits to an individual are worth more than the total cost. These privileged groups have no need to rely on ideology or personal loyalty to produce the needed contributions because a personal interest, not simply a collective one, already exists for at least some people.

Note that this argument actually applies to the size of the constituency rather than the size of the challenging group itself. None of the 53 groups could really be considered small in this sense. Even those that failed to mobilize many were aiming at a substantial group. But size is, anyway, only a rather crude indicator of a privileged group and not a defining characteristic. Some large groups may have individuals who value the change sought by the group enough to pay the full cost or, at least, to make up any deficit not provided by the constituency. Many smaller groups may lack such individuals.

Not all of the challenging groups in this study began life friendless. About one-fourth of them (14) enjoyed the patronage of some individual or group with significant power or wealth. Although these groups, by definition, were also attempting to mobilize a constituency, they were not as completely dependent on this constituency for resources as an unsponsored group was. The American Committee for the Outlawry of War, for example, enjoyed the patronage of an energetic and well-connected lawyer, Salmon O. Levinson. In many ways, the committee was a vehicle for Levinson's crusade. He made sporadic efforts to raise money from others but without much success. At one point, he "tried charging a small price for printed material that he had been sending out gratis, especially when large batches were called for. But when Amy Woods of the Women's International League for Peace and Freedom asked for fifty thousand pamphlets and insisted that there was no money to pay for them, he made an exception. In point of fact, exceptions were made in nearly every case, so that very little money was raised from that source" (Stoner, 1942, p. 108). Levinson did not have unlimited personal funds and made plaintive pleas for help from rich angels but without success.

Engrossed as he was in the campaign, Levinson "really never made any but scattered and sporadic attempts to raise money. He much preferred to give what was needed out of his own pocket rather than be distracted from his main object. . . . He began to pay more than 95 percent of the expense of the campaign out of his own pocket, and he continued to do so even when it was costing upward of fifteen thousand dollars annually" (Stoner, pp. 108–110).

In addition to this kind of personal sponsorship, there is organizational sponsorship. The fledgling Steel Workers Organizing Committee did not have to depend on its nascent membership for the resources it needed to carry on its battles with the steel producers. The CIO was ready to lend its help. "[John L.] Lewis had given us a check for $25,000," David McDonald explained, "[but] that barely got our office open. The task of putting together an effective group of organizers was the heart of our effort. It was also expensive, and Lewis knew it. Within a few weeks, he sent us a second check, this time for $500,000" (McDonald, 1969, p. 91). When it came time to select quarters, McDonald chose a suite "on the thirty-sixth floor of the Grant Building—Pittsburgh's tallest at that time—[which] looked out splendidly over the industrial heart of the city. It also topped by several floors offices of some of the steel companies we hoped to organize and left no doubt of our permanence and stability. . . . The word got around quickly in the right places that this was no fly-by-night effort but a well-financed movement of labor union professionals who knew what they were about and meant business" (McDonald, p. 91).

Sponsorship, then, is an indicator of a privileged group. Someone or some organization has a special concern for the cause and resources to back up their concern. Such a challenger is no happier with free-riders than anyone else and is anxious to draw needed resources from its constituency. But it can tolerate a greater number of free-riders given the presence of a few highly committed, well-paying passengers.

Figure 5–2 indicates that privileged groups are only very slightly more successful than the others—57 percent against slightly less

FIGURE 5–2
Privilege or Sponsorship by Outcome

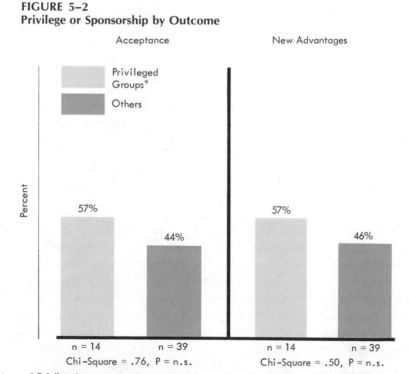

* Privileged groups are those with rich and/or powerful patrons. To be included, resources of the patron or sponsor must have existed prior to the challenge and not have resulted from the challenge itself.

than half of the rest. There is, however, some indication of an interaction between sponsorship and size in determining success. Overall, privileged groups are no different in size from the rest — half are over 10,000 and half are under. But the successful privileged groups tend to be a little smaller than the others. Only one of the eight successful ones grew to over 100,000 (the Steel Workers Organizing Committee) while half of the six unsuccessful privileged groups achieved this size. There is at least a suggestion here that sponsorship has more of an impact with groups of smaller size, but that its effects are dissipated when the group is beyond a certain magnitude.

SELECTIVE INCENTIVES

The core of Olson's argument for overcoming the free-rider problem is the "by-product" theory of the production of collective goods.

> The common characteristic which distinguishes all of the large economic groups with significant lobbying organizations is that these groups are also organized for some *other* purpose. The large and powerful economic lobbies are in fact the by-products of organizations that obtain their strength and support because they perform some function in addition to lobbying for collective goods.
>
> The lobbies of the large economic groups are the by-products of organizations that have the capacity to "mobilize" a latent group with "selective incentives." The only organizations that have the "selective incentives" available are those that (1) have the authority and capacity to be coercive, or (2) have a source of positive inducements that they can offer the individuals in a latent group (Olson, pp. 132–33).

Challenging groups are, by definition, organized for the purpose of producing a collective good and not for some other purpose. If a group organized for the purpose of providing some benefit or service to members and, once well-established, took on a new cause, it would not be included here. I suspect that Olson has an important insight in recognizing the advantage that such groups possess in separating the problems of mobilization and social influence. Challenging groups, in contrast, face the problems simultaneously; they seek changes from an antagonist and support from a constituency at the same time.

We cannot compare challenging groups with groups organized

for other purposes because we have no sample of the latter. But we can examine the use of selective incentives among challenging groups and compare those that used them with those that did not. Challenging group leaders were not unaware of the need for selective incentives, and one of them formulated the issues 75 years ago in a form not very different from Olson's argument. Henry Crowther, of the League of American Wheelmen, addressed the question "How to Increase the League Membership" in an article in *Good Roads Magazine* in the 1890s.

> It will, I think, be universally admitted that the average man (and it has not yet been discovered that the average wheelman is built on a different plan from the ordinary citizen) in nowise attempts to conceal his anxiety to know what he gets out of anything he is solicited to "go into," whether it be a real estate deal, stock-jobbing operation, secret society, or beneficial or fraternal organization—and justly so. The quid pro quo obtains in all our dealings from the cradle to the grave. . . . During a period extending over something like ten years of League work, my experience has almost invariably been . . . that the first question broached by a rider, when requested to join the L.A.W., is "What do I get out of it?" And, mind you, he is usually quite deaf to any sentimental arguments. The benefits of fellowship with the thirty-odd thousand of us who go to make up the elect have no weight with him. He wants—and justly so, again—to see paid down to him in hand the material benefits. . . . This being the case, what is to do? Why, give it to him, of course. Herein lies, in a nutshell, the secret of that future growth of the organization which can make the League of American Wheelmen that power in the land which it can become under properly directed effort. . . . Pennsylvania owes no small measure of her growth to the fine road books which are furnished to her members free . . . in addition to the weekly paper which each one of them receives.

The League of American Wheelmen was not the only group to offer private inducements to its members as selective incentives for joining. Eight others did also, including some unions that emphasized private benefits as well as collective ones. The Sons of Vulcan, for example, emphasized "aid to sick and distressed members." The Amalgamated Association of Street and Electrical Railway Employees of America maintained a death and disability benefit system, as did the United Brotherhood of Carpenters and Joiners of America.

In addition to these nine that offered selective inducements to members, two more made use of selective incentives of a negative sort. David McDonald describes the early problems of making the emerging steelworkers union solvent. "In the first glow of the U.S. Steel and J&L [Jones and Laughlin] victories, it seemed that our financial problems were finally at an end. Dues from our new members in these companies would make us solvent and perhaps even permit us to put a little aside to apply on our debt to the United Mine Workers. All of this would have been true if the steelworkers had paid their dollar-a-month dues. But once in, the great majority of them simply ignored their dues. We were suddenly rich in members and starved for funds" (McDonald, 1969, p. 108).

While dues check-off offered an ultimate answer, McDonald judged it impossible to gain agreement from the steel industry at that point in the struggle. The technique adopted to collect dues was something "we called . . . visual education, which was a high-sounding label for a practice much more accurately described as dues picketing. It worked very simply. A group of dues-paying members, selected by the district director (usually more for their size than their tact) would stand at the plant gate with pick handles or baseball bats in hand and confront each worker as he arrived for his shift" (p. 121).

While steelworkers confronted the pick handle, tobacco growers who resisted the Night Riders faced the whip or worse. Holdouts were terrorized by activities that "included the writing of threatening letters; the destruction of plantbeds; the burning of barns and other buildings; whippings; night visits to farmers to warn them or leave threatening notes; shooting scrapes; and the destruction of such other property as farm machinery, grain, hay, livestock, steam engines, sawmills, and wheat-threshing outfits. . . . The majority of growers . . . who received notes or night visits from the Night Riders, obeyed their orders as soon as convenient" (Nall, 1939, pp. 115–17).

All 53 groups attempted persuasion as a means of mobilization. All attempted to appeal to values or group loyalty to recruit potential members. The 11 groups that make use of selective incentives differ from the others, not in ignoring appeals to solidarity but in going beyond such appeals. Thus, we are contrasting groups that rely *only* on some form of persuasion with those that make use of some form of inducement or constraint as well.

Figure 5–3 provides clear support for the Olson hypothesis. All but one (91 percent) of the selective incentive groups won acceptance, and all but two (82 percent) won new advantages contrasted with, respectively, 36 percent and 40 percent of the others. The only exception to acceptance was the Night Riders, and, as indicated earlier, the allied Planters Protective Association achieved this in their stead. The exceptions to winning new advantages were two co-opted groups, the Dairymen's League and the Seamen's Union. Both of these groups developed cozy relationships with their "antagonists" and continued to exist after the end of the challenge and to maintain or, in one case, even increase their membership. That they were able to do this at the same time they were failing to deliver any real collective benefits to their constituency may well have been due to their use of selective inducements to membership.

There is another relevant fact about the selective incentive

FIGURE 5-3
Selective Incentives by Outcome

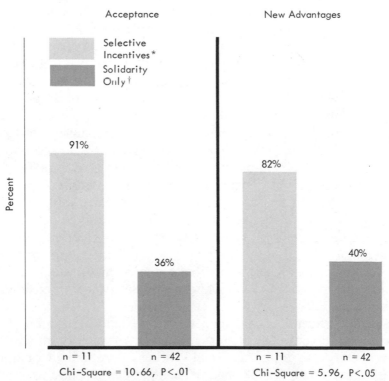

* Groups that provide selective incentives to members in addition to attempting mobilization on the basis of loyalty or solidarity.
† Groups that rely only on appeals to loyalty or solidarity.

groups — they tended to be large. Seventy-three percent of them reached a membership of over 100,000 while only 16 percent of the remainder did so. Put another way, large groups were not notably successful without selective incentives. Of those over 100,000, only two of seven won new advantages without selective incentives, and only three of seven won acceptance. For groups of this size with selective incentives, six of eight won new advantages and all won acceptance. In short, groups may grow large without the use of selective incentives, but, in their absence, they have difficulty converting size into success.

SUMMARY

There is much in this chapter to suggest the relevance of the theory of public goods for understanding challenging groups. The logic of collective action suggests that those groups that appeal to members in terms of their common interest have the same fundamental problem as universalistic groups. The data here provide no particular reason to doubt this.

Privileged groups, in the theory, should have at least a partial immunity to the free-rider problem. Overall, these privileged groups do not fare much better than the others, but there does seem to be some effect when the privileged group remains small. Even though many potential members fail to join these smaller groups, the intense support of a few is apparently able to compensate for lack of numbers. With the larger groups who have managed somehow to overcome the problem of free-riders, the help of rich or powerful sponsors is largely irrelevant in determining outcome.

In lieu of sponsors, large groups do particularly well when they employ selective incentives, and selective incentives help a group to grow large. Eight of 11 groups employing selective incentives gained more than 100,000 members, and, whether large or moderate in size, all 11 achieved at least one form of success. Large groups that relied only on loyalty or solidarity were considerably less successful.

Selective incentives and sponsorship serve as alternative means of meeting the basic problem suggested by the theory of collective action. Only one group, the Steel Workers Organizing Committee, had both. There were 29 groups that had neither, and only about one-third of these (10) were able to win new advantages with even fewer (8) winning acceptance. Thus, it is not impossible to succeed with only loyalty and solidarity as one's mobilization weapon, but the reduced success rate of such groups supports the usefulness of the theory of collective goods in understanding the careers of these challengers.

REFERENCES

Coleman, James S. "Loss of Power." *American Sociological Review,* February 1973, 38:1–17.

Gamson, William A. *Power and Discontent.* Homewood, Ill.: Dorsey, 1968.

Hirschman, Albert. *Exit, Voice, and Loyalty.* Cambridge, Mass.: Harvard University Press, 1970.

Lenin, V. I. *What Is to Be Done?* New York: International Publishers, 1929.

McDonald, David J. *Union Man.* New York: Dutton, 1969.

Nall, J. O. *Tobacco Night Riders of Kentucky and Tennessee, 1905–1909.* Louisville, Ky.: Standard Press, 1939.

Olson, Mancur, Jr. *The Logic of Collective Action.* Cambridge, Mass.: Harvard University Press, 1965.

Stoner, John E. *S. O. Levinson and the Pact of Paris.* Chicago: University of Chicago Press, 1942.

chapter six

The Success of the Unruly

It is a happy fact that we continue to be shocked by the appearance of violence in social protest. Apparently, frequency is no great cushion against shock for, at least in America, social protest has been liberally speckled with violent episodes. One can exaggerate the frequency—a majority of challenges run their course without any history of violence or arrests. But a very substantial minority—more than 25 percent—have violence in their history. The fact that violence is a common consort of social protest in the United States is not a matter of serious contention.

The consequences of violence are at issue. It is commonly believed to be self-defeating. Evaluating the validity of this belief is made elusive by a tendency that we all have, social scientists and laymen alike, to allow our moral judgments to influence our strategic judgments and vice versa. Kaplowitz has suggested the following general hypothesis. If strategic rationality does not clearly specify a course of action as desirable but normative criteria do,

---

Earlier versions of this chapter were presented at the annual meeting of the Israel Sociological Society at Bar Ilan University, January, 1973, and the American Sociological Association in New York, August, 1973.

people will tend to believe that the normatively desirable course of action is also strategically rational.[1]

Violence is relatively unambiguous morally. At most, it is regarded as a necessary evil which may be justified in preventing or overcoming some even greater evil. And for many, the situations in which it is justified are scant to nonexistent. The issue depends on one's image of the society in which violence takes place. In a closed and oppressive political system that offers no nonviolent means for accomplishing change, the morality of violence is not as clear. But when it is believed that effective nonviolent alternatives exist, almost everybody would consider these morally preferable.

In the pluralist image of American society, the political system is relatively open, offering access at many points for effective nonviolent protest and efforts at change. With this premise, the use of violence by groups engaged in efforts at social change seems particularly reprehensible. The above reasoning should apply not only to violence as a means of influence but as a means of social control as well. The use of violence and other extralegal methods for dealing with protestors is also morally reprehensible.

While the moral issues may be clear, the strategic ones are ambiguous. There is no consensus on the set of conditions under which violence is a more or less effective strategy, and the issue has been seriously analyzed only in the international sphere. The Kaplowitz hypothesis, if correct, explains the strong tendency for people to believe that something so immoral as domestic violence is not a very effective strategy in domestic social protest. It also helps us to recognize that the fact that many people regard violence as self-defeating is no evidence that it is actually futile.

The pluralist view, then, acknowledges that collective violence has taken place in the United States with considerable frequency but argues that it is effective neither as a strategy of social influence when used by challenging groups nor as a strategy of repression when it is used by the enemies of such groups. We treat this view here as an hypothesis. It would be comforting to find that moral and strategic imperatives coincide, but the evidence discussed below suggests that they do not.

---

[1] Kaplowitz has explored the interaction between normative and strategic criteria experimentally (1973). He also argues for the complementary hypothesis to the one stated above: If normative criteria do not clearly specify a course of action while strategic criteria do, people will tend to believe that the strategically rational choice is the more normative one.

VIOLENCE USERS AND RECIPIENTS

I mean by the term "violence" deliberate physical injury to property or persons. This does not embrace such things as forceful constraint — for example, arrest — unless it is accompanied by beatings or other physical injury. It also excludes bribery, brainwashing, and other nasty techniques. To use the term violence as a catch-all for unpleasant means of influence or social control confuses the issue; other unpopular means need to stand forth on their own for evaluation, and we will explore some of these as well.

Among the 53 groups, there were 15 that engaged in violent interactions with antagonists, agents of social control, or hostile third parties. Eight of these groups were active participants; they themselves used violence. It is important to emphasize that these "violence users" were not necessarily initiators; in some cases they were attacked and fought back, and in still others the sequence of events is unclear. No assumption is made that the violence users were necessarily the aggressors in the violent interaction that transpired.

Whether they initiate violence or not, all of the violence users accept it, some with reluctance and some with apparent glee. Wallace Stegner (1949, pp. 255–56) describes some of the actions of Father Coughlin's Christian Front against Communism. "In Boston, a *Social Justice* truck went out to distribute the paper without benefit of the mails. When a *Boston Traveler* photographer tried for a picture, the truck driver kicked his camera apart while a friendly cop held the photographer's arms." In another incident in the Boston area, a printer named Levin was approached by Christian Fronters who handed him *Social Justice* and told him, " 'Here, you're a Jew, Levin. You ought to read about what your pals have been doing lately. Take a look how your investments in Russia are coming.' . . . One morning, . . . Levin came down to his shop to find it broken open and its contents wrecked." In New York, as Stegner describes it (p. 252), Christian Fronters would start fights with passing Jews, would beat up one or two opponents, and then vanish. Another source, Charles Tull (1965, p. 207) writes, that "it was common for the Coughlinite pickets . . . to be involved in violence with their more vocal critics. . . . Street brawls involving Christian Fronters and Jews became frequent in New York City. . . ." Now these accounts are at best unsympathetic to the Christian Front. Some of the clashes may well have been initiated by opponents of the group. For example, Tull points out that the "most notable incident from the standpoint of sheer numbers occurred on April 8, 1939, when a crowd of several thousand people mobbed ten newsboys selling *Social Justice*." Although the Christian Fronters may have been passive recipients of violence in this particular case, on many other occasions they clearly played the role of active participant or more.

The active role is even clearer in the case of the Tobacco Night Riders. Earlier (Chapter Five, p. 68), I discussed violence directed against their constituency, but much of their violence was directed at the tobacco trust as well. "The Tobacco Night Riders were organized in 1906 as a secret, fraternal order, officially called 'The Silent Brigade' or 'The Inner Circle.' Their purpose was to force all growers to join the [Planters Protective] Association . . . and to force the [tobacco] trust companies to buy tobacco only from the association" (Nall, 1942).

The violence of the Night Riders was the most organized of any group studied. They "made their first show of armed force at Princeton [Kentucky], on the morning of Saturday, December 1, 1906 when shortly after midnight approximately 250 armed and masked men took possession of the city and dynamited and burned two large tobacco factories. . . . Citizens in the business district opened windows and looked out on bodies of masked men hurrying along with guns on their shoulders. They saw other masked and armed men patrolling the sidewalks and street corners and they heard commands: 'Get back!' And if they did not obey, bullets splattered against the brick walls near by or crashed through the window panes above their heads. . . . Several squads of men had marched in along the Cadiz road and captured the police station, the waterworks plants, the courthouse, and the telephone and telegraph offices. They had disarmed the policemen and put them under guard, shut off the city water supply, and taken the places of the telephone and telegraph operators. . . . Within a few minutes the city was in control of the Riders and all communication with the outside was cut off." With their mission accomplished and the tobacco factories in flames, the men "mounted their horses and rode away singing 'The fire shines bright in my old Kentucky home' " (Nall, 1942, p. 69).

About a year later, the Night Riders struck again at the town of Hopkinsville, Kentucky. It is worth noting, since the argument here views violence as instrumental rather than expressive, that the

Hopkinsville raid was twice postponed when it appeared that the town was prepared to resist. "The Night Riders were not cowards," Nall writes, "but their cause and methods of operation did not demand that they face a resistant line of shot and shell to accomplish their purposes." The Night Riders made heavy use of fifth columnists in the town to assure that their raid could be successful without bloodshed. As in the Princeton raid, they carried out the operation with precision, occupying all strategic points. During this raid, they "shot into the . . . residence of W. Lindsay Mitchell, a buyer for the Imperial Tobacco Company, shattering electric lights and windowpanes. A group entered the house and disarmed him just in time to keep him from shooting into their comrades. He was brought into the street and struck over the head several times with a gun barrel, sustaining painful wounds. The captain of the squad looked on until he considered that Mr. Mitchell had 'had enough' then rescued him and escorted him back to his door" (Nall, p. 78). After the raid, they reassembled out of town for a roll call and marched away singing. The sheriff and local military officer organized a small posse to pursue the raiders and attacked their rear, killing one man and wounding another before the posse was forced to retreat back to Hopkinsville. One might have thought that the Night Riders would have retaliated for the attack made on them by the posse, and, indeed, Nall reports that "some of the Riders considered a second raid to retaliate . . . but such was not considered by the leaders. They had accomplished their purpose" (p. 82).

The Native American, or American Republican Party, a nativist group of the 1840s, was heavily implicated in less organized violence directed against Catholics. "Traversing the Irish section [of Philadelphia], the [nativist] mob was soon locked in armed conflict with equally riotous foreigners. The Hibernia Hose Company house was stormed and demolished; before midnight, more than thirty houses belonging to Irishmen had been burned to the ground. . . ." A few nights later, "roaming the streets, the rioters finally came to Saint Michael's Catholic Church. A rumor that arms were concealed within the building proved sufficient grounds for attack, and while the presiding priest fled in disguise, the torch was applied. . . ." The mob also burned St. Augustine's Church and "throughout the city, priests and nuns trembled for their lives" (Billington, 1963, pp. 225–26). Party leadership repudiated much of this mob action but especially deplored and emphasized the counterattacks: "the killing of natives by foreign mobs." The central involvement of American Republicans was, however, substantial and well-documented.

The other violence users were all labor unions involved in clashes with strikebreakers or police and militia called out to assist and defend the strikebreakers. Among the violence users, then, the challenging group is sometimes the initiator but not always; sometimes the leadership openly defends and advocates the practice but not always. To be classified as a violence user, it is only necessary that the group be an active participant in the violent interactions in which it is involved.

The recipients of violence were passive recipients — they were attacked and either did not or, because they had insufficient means, could not fight back. The International Workingmen's Association, the First International, is one example. In September, 1873, a major financial panic occurred in the United States, resulting in subsequent unemployment and economic dislocation. A mass demonstration was called for January 13, 1874, in the form of a march of the unemployed in New York City. To quote John Commons (1966, p. 220), "It was the original plan of the Committee that the parade should disband after a mass meeting in front of the city hall but this was prohibited by the authorities and Tompkins Square was chosen as the next best place for the purpose. The parade was formed at the appointed hour and by the time it reached Tompkins Square it had swelled to an immense procession. Here they were met by a force of policemen and, immediately after the order to disperse had been given, the police charged with drawn clubs. During the ensuing panic, hundreds of workmen were injured."

Abolitionists were frequent recipients of violence in the form of antiabolitionist riots. The object of the violence was primarily the property and meeting places of abolitionists rather than their persons, although there were frequent threats and some physical abuse as well. The National Female Anti-Slavery Society was victimized on various occasions, although the women themselves were never attacked. Once, when the hall in which they were scheduled to hold a meeting was set on fire by an antiabolitionist mob, the women sought refuge in the home of Lucretia Mott. "As the rioters swarmed through nearby streets, it seemed as if an attack on the Mott house were imminent but a friend of the Motts joined the mob, and crying, 'On to the Motts' led them in the wrong direction" (Lutz, 1968, p. 139). William Lloyd Garrison was attacked at one of the meetings and dragged through the streets. The American Anti-Slavery Society was similarly abused. Eggs and stones were thrown at the audience of several of their meetings. In Cincinnati, rioters attacked the shops and homes of abolitionists, particularly Englishmen. An abolitionist printer in Illinois, Elijah Lovejoy, was killed when he attempted to resist an antiabolitionist mob destroying his shop. Lovejoy's resistance was isolated and provoked a controversy in the fervently nonviolent Society. Lovejoy had had his printing presses destroyed three times, "his house was invaded, and his wife was brought to the verge of hysterical collapse. When a fourth new press arrived, Lovejoy determined that he would protect it. . . . When his press was attacked he raised his pistol but was quickly gunned down by one of the mob." Even under such circumstances, "abolitionists in the American Anti-Slavery Society and elsewhere were divided on whether or not to censure Lovejoy's action" (Sorin, 1972, p. 91). They did not censure Lovejoy but reasserted their commitment to nonviolent means of achieving the end of slavery.

Members of the National Student League were attacked in the familiar manner of northern civil rights workers going south in the 1960s. In one instance, the cause was the bitter struggle of coal miners in Harlan County, Kentucky. "At Cumberland Gap, the mountain pass into Kentucky, the full impact of Kentucky law and order descended. The road was almost dark when the bus turned the corner over the boundary; out of the approaching night the scowling faces of a mob of more than 200 people greeted the visitors. Cars drove up and surrounded the bus; most of the throng were armed, wearing the badges of deputy sheriffs. . . . There were derisive cat-calls, then the ominous lynch-cry: 'String 'em up' " (Wechsler, 1935). Students were shoved and some knocked down, but none seriously injured on this occasion.

The recipients of violence, then, unlike the users, play essentially passive roles in the violent episodes in which they were involved. The success or failure of the violence users will enable us to say something about the effectiveness of violence as a means of influence; the success or failure of the violence recipients will help us to evelute the effectiveness of violence as a means of social control.

THE RESULTS

What is the fate of these groups? Are the users of violence crushed by adverse public reaction and the coercive power of the state? Do the recipients of violence rouse the public sympathy with their martyrdom, rallying to their cause important bystanders who are appalled at their victimization and join them in their struggle?

FIGURE 6–1
Violence and Outcome

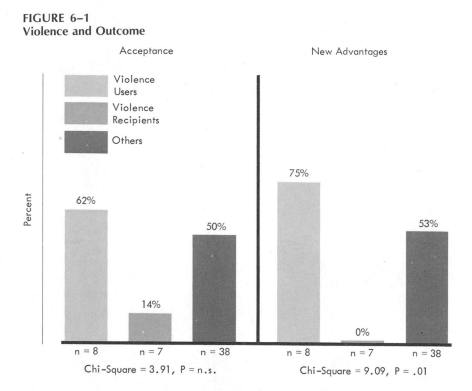

Figure 6–1 gives the basic results. The violence users, it turns out, have a higher-than-average success rate. Six of the eight won new advantages, and five of these six established a minimal acceptance relationship as well. Of course, some paid their dues in blood in the process as we have seen in the descriptions above. The seven recipients of violence also paid such dues but with little or nothing to show for it in the end. One, The Dairymen's League, established a minimal acceptance relationship with its antagonist, but none of them were able to gain new advantages for their benefi-

ciary. With respect to violence and success, it appears better to give than receive.

It is worth asking whether the different goals of these groups might account for the difference. The most relevant variable, as we learned in Chapter Four, is whether the displacement of the antagonist is part of the goals. Two of the eight violence users have displacement goals, and two of the seven violence recipients do also. Figure 6–2 makes the same comparison as Figure 6–1 but only for those groups that are not attempting to replace their targets. It reveals that every violence user with more limited goals is successful, although the Night Riders were not accepted; every violence recipient was unsuccessful, although the Dairymen's League won minimal acceptance. The earlier result is, if anything, sharpened.

FIGURE 6–2
Violence and Outcome Excluding Displacing Groups

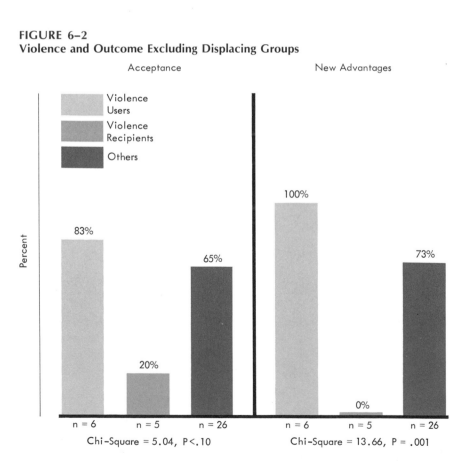

DOES VIOLENCE PAY?

Am I ready to conclude then that violence basically works? Not quite, or at least not in any simple fashion, and my caution is not due simply to the small number of cases involved and the real possibility of sampling error. It is easier to say what these data refute than what they prove.

Specifically, the data undermine the following line of thinking: violence is the product of frustration, desperation, and weakness. It is an act of last resort by those who see no other means of achieving their goals. In this view, the challenging group, frustrated by its inability to attract a significant following and gain some response from its targets of influence, turns to violence in desperation. However, this merely hastens and insures its failure because its actions increase the hostility around it and invite the legitimate action of authorities against it.

When authorities use violence against challenging groups, there are similar dynamics in this argument. Frightened by the growing strength of the challenging group and unable to halt its rising power by legitimate means, tottering on their throne and unwilling to make concessions, the threatened authorities turn to repression. But this attempted repression simply adds fuel to the fire, bringing new allies to the cause of the challenging group and increasing its chances of ultimate success.

However compelling these images may be, they clearly do not fit the data presented here. The interpretation I would suggest is almost the opposite. As Eisinger (1973) puts it in discussing protest behavior in American cities, one hypothesis is that protest is as much a "signal of impatience as frustration." Violence should be viewed as an instrumental act, aimed at furthering the purposes of the group that uses it when they have some reason to think it will help their cause. This is especially likely to be true when the normal condemnation which attends to its use is muted or neutralized in the surrounding community, when it is tacitly condoned by large parts of the audience. In this sense, it grows from an impatience born of confidence and rising efficacy rather than the opposite. It occurs when hostility toward the victim renders it a relatively safe and costless strategy. The users of violence sense that they will be exonerated because they will be seen as more the midwives than the initiators of punishment. The victims are implicitly told, "See how your sins have provoked the wrath of the fanatics and have brought this punishment upon yourselves."

The size of the violence users and recipients supports this interpretation. The violence users tend to be large groups, the recipients small ones. Only one of the eight violence users is under 10,000 (the Night Riders) while five of the seven violence recipients are this small. Such growth seems more likely to breed confidence and impatience, not desperation.

I am arguing, then, that it is not the weakness of the user but the weakness of the target that accounts for violence. This is not to say that the weakness of a target is sufficient to produce violence but that, in making it more likely to be profitable, it makes it more likely to occur. As Figure 6–2 showed, many challenging groups are able to gain a positive response without resorting to violence, and many collapse without the added push of repression. But groups that are failing for other reasons and authorities that are being forced to respond by rising pressures generally do not turn to violence. This is why, in my interpretation, violence is associated with successful change or successful repression: it grows out of confidence and strength and their attendant impatience with the pace of change. It is, in this sense, as much a symptom of success as a cause.

It is worth noting that, with the exception of the Night Riders, none of the groups that used violence made it a primary tactic. Typically it was incidental to the primary means of influence — strikes, bargaining, propaganda, or other nonviolent means. It is the spice, not the meat and potatoes. And, if one considers the Night Riders as merely the striking arm of the respectable Planters Protective Association, even this exception is no exception.

The groups that receive violence, with one exception, are attacked in an atmosphere of countermobilization of which the physical attacks are the cutting edge. They are attacked not merely because they are regarded as threatening — all challenging groups are threatening to some vested interest. They are threatening *and* vulnerable, and most fail to survive the physical attacks to which they are subjected.

OTHER CONSTRAINTS

This argument can be further evaluated by extending it to other constraints in addition to violence. "Constraints are the addition of new disadvantages to the situation or the threat to do so, regardless of the particular resources used" (Gamson, 1968). Violence is a special case of constraints but there are many others.

Twenty-one groups (40 percent) made use of constraints as a means of influence in pursuing their challenge. We have already considered eight of them, those that used violence, and we turn now to the other 13. The most common constraints used by these groups were strikes and boycotts, but they also included such things as efforts to discredit and humiliate individual enemies by personal vituperation. Discrediting efforts directed against "the system" or other more abstract targets are not included, but only individualized, ad hominem attacks attempting to injure personal reputation.

Included here, for example, is A. Philip Randolph's March on Washington Committee, designed to push President Roosevelt into a more active role in ending discrimination in employment. A mass march in the spring of 1941 to protest racial discrimination in America would have been a considerable embarrassment to the Roosevelt administration. America was mobilizing for war behind appeals that contrasted democracy with the racism of the Nazi regime. Walter White of the NAACP described "the President's skillful attempts to dissuade us" (Quoted in Garfinkel, 1969). The march was, from the standpoint of the administration, something to be avoided, a new disadvantage which the committee was threatening.

William Randolph Hearst's Independence League made liberal use of personal vituperation against opponents. "Most of Hearst's energy was devoted to pointing out the personal inequities of boss Charles F. Murphy. He found himself obliged to go back to the time of Tweed to discover any parallel in political corruption. . . . 'Murphy is as evil a specimen of a criminal boss as we have had since the days of Tweed' " (Carlson and Bates, 1936, pp. 146–47).

The League of Deliverance made primary use of the boycott weapon, employing it against businesses that hired Chinese labor. They threatened worse. The League's executive committee proposed to notify offenders of their desires and if not complied with, "after the expiration of six days it will be the duty of the Executive Committee to declare the district dangerous . . . . Should the Chinese remain within the proclaimed district after the expiration of . . . thirty days, the general Executive Committee will be required to abate the danger in whatever manner seems best to them" (Cross, 1935). The League, however, never had call to go beyond the boycott tactic.

Among the 13 nonviolent constraint users are three groups that were considered earlier as violence recipients. Including them makes it more difficult to interpret the relationship of success to the use of constraints since this is compounded by physical attacks on the group. Therefore, in Figure 6–3, we include only those ten groups that employed constraints but were not involved in violent interactions as either user or recipient. The advantage again goes to the unruly. Four-fifths of the constraint users and only two-fifths of the others are successful.

Constraints other than violence can also be used as a means of social control. In particular, many groups experience arrest and imprisonment or deportation of members which can be equally as devastating as physical attack, if not more so. Almost two-fifths of

FIGURE 6–3
Constraints and Outcome

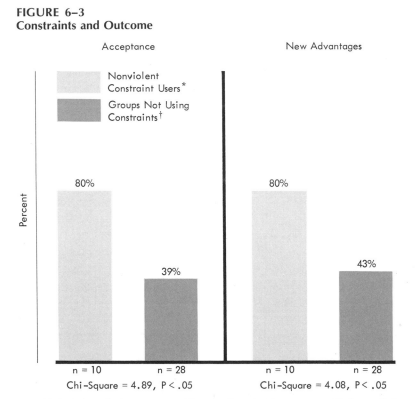

* This includes only those groups making use of constraints as a means of influence that were not involved in violent interactions as either users or recipients.

† This excludes groups that did not use constraints if they were also violence recipients.

the sample (20 groups) had members arrested at some time or another during the period of challenge. These twenty included all eight of the violence users and four of the seven recipients, leaving only eight groups that were not involved in violent interactions but were subjected to arrests.

The Young Peoples Socialist League had people arrested during both its periods of challenge. " 'You're under arrest' " began an article in *The Challenge,* the YPSL paper. "This was not the first time members of the Young Peoples Socialist League had heard this pronouncement by officers while they were peacefully demonstrating against injustice." During its period of challenge in the World War I era, the national secretary of the group, William Kruse, was arrested, tried, convicted, and sentenced to 20 years imprisonment but ultimately won on appeal.

The German-American Bund was subject to arrests on a number of occasions. Fritz Kuhn, the group's major leader, was convicted of embezzling Bund funds, income tax evasion, and forgery. Other members were indicted on more political charges such as espionage. Some were tried in New York State under a rarely invoked statute passed in 1923 as a measure against the Ku Klux Klan, but Bundists won on appeal (Rowan, 1939, p. 178).

The American Birth Control League also experienced its share of official harassment. Soon after its organization, Margaret Sanger arrived at Town Hall in New York with her featured speaker, Harold Cox, editor of the *Edinburgh Review.*

> She found a crowd gathered outside. One hundred policemen, obviously intending to prevent the meeting, ringed the locked doors of the hall. When the police opened the doors to let people already inside exit, those outside rushed in, carrying Mrs. Sanger and Cox before them. Once inside, Mrs. Sanger tried several times to speak, but policemen forcibly removed her from the platform. . . . Cox managed only to blurt, "I have come across the Atlantic to address you," before two policemen hauled him from the stage. The police arrested Mrs. Sanger and led her out of the hall while the audience sang, "My country, 'Tis of Thee."

A few weeks later, with evidence of complicity of the Catholic Church in the raid emerging, Mrs. Juliet Barrett Rublee, a friend of Mrs. Sanger, was arrested "while she was in the act of testifying at an investigation into the charge of church influence behind the [earlier] raid" (Kennedy, 1970, pp. 95–96).

Figure 6–4 considers the eight groups subjected to arrest, again

FIGURE 6–4
Arrests and Outcome

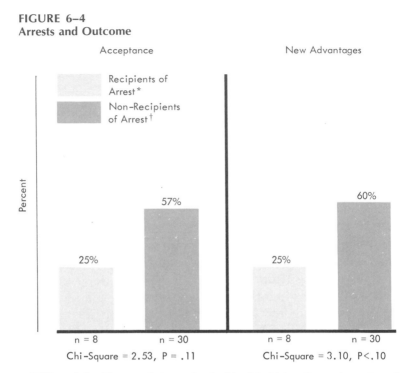

Acceptance   New Advantages

* This excludes 12 groups that were involved in violent interactions and experienced arrests.

† This excludes 3 groups that were involved in violent interactions but did not experience arrests.

excluding all groups involved in violent interactions.[2] Only two of the eight groups were successful while nearly 60 percent of the remainder were. The results seem even clearer when we examine the two exceptions. Only two of the eight groups made use of non-violent constraints – the League of Deliverance used the boycott and the United Brotherhood of Carpenters and Joiners of America used strikes and boycotts. These two groups were the only successes among the eight groups considered in Figure 6–4. In other words, groups that used neither violence nor any other form of constraint and yet experienced arrest were uniformly unsuccessful. In the absence of offsetting tactics by challenging groups, arrest seems to have the same connection with outcome as receiving violence, both are associated with failure for the receiving group.

---

[2] Only three of the 15 groups involved in violent interactions escaped arrests, all violence recipients. The violence in these cases came from hostile third parties – for example, anti-abolitionist mobs – and the perpetrators of violence also escaped arrest.

There is another interesting fact about the six groups in Figure 6–4 that experience both arrests and failure. Five out of the six were attempting to displace antagonists as part of their goals, and three of the six advocated violence in principle even though they never actually employed it. Eisinger points out that "as long as protestors do not manipulate the threat of violence explicitly, they enjoy a slim legality, even, occasionally, legitimacy. Once they employ the threat openly, however, they open the way for authorities to suppress their movement or action" (1973, p. 14).

Groups like the Communist Labor Party, the Revolutionary Workers League, and the German-American Bund put themselves in the position of advocating or accepting violence as a tactic without actually using it. One might call this the strategy of speaking loudly and carrying a small stick. These groups seem to pay the cost of violence without gaining the benefits of employing it. They are both threatening and weak, and their repression becomes a low-cost strategy for those whom they attempt to displace.

SUMMARY

The results on arrests and other constraints seem to parallel those on violence very closely. Unruly groups, those that use violence, strikes, and other constraints, have better than average success. Of the 21 groups that use some form of constraint, fully two-thirds win new advantages and 71 percent win acceptance. Among the ten groups that use no constraints but receive either violence or arrests, none are successful on either criterion. The 22 groups that neither experience nor use constraints fall in the middle, 54 percent (12) win new advantages and half win acceptance.

Virtue, of course, has its own, intrinsic rewards. And a lucky thing it does too, since its instrumental value appears to be dubious. If we cannot say with certainty that violence and other constraints are successful tactics of social influence or social control, we must at least have greater doubt about the proposition that they lead to failure. When used by challenging groups, there is no evidence that they close doors that are open to those who use only inducements and persuasion. When used against challenging groups, there is no evidence that such tactics bring allies and sympathetic third parties to the effective aid of the beleaguered groups, allowing them to gain what would have been impossible acting alone.

Perhaps it is disconcerting to discover that restraint is not rewarded with success. But those who use more unruly tactics escape misfortune because they are clever enough to use these tactics primarily in situations where public sentiment neutralizes the normal deviance of the action, thus reducing the likelihood and effectiveness of counterattack.

REFERENCES

Billington, Ray Allen. *The Protestant Crusade, 1800–1860.* Gloucester, Mass.: P. Smith, 1963.

Carlson, Oliver and Bates, Ernest S. *Hearst, Lord of San Simeon.* New York: Viking Press, 1936.

Commons, John R. et al., *History of Labor in the United States,* Vol. II. New York: A. M. Kelley, 1966.

Cross, Ira B. *A History of the Labor Movement in California.* Berkeley, California: University of California Press, 1935.

Eisinger, Peter K. "The Conditions of Protest Behavior in American Cities." *American Political Science Review,* March, 1973, 67:11–28.

Gamson, William A. *Power and Discontent.* Homewood, Ill.: Dorsey Press, 1968.

Garfinkel, Herbert. *When Negroes March.* New York: Atheneum, 1969.

Kaplowitz, Stan. "An Experimental Test of a Rationalistic Theory of Deterence." *Journal of Conflict Resolution,* September, 1973, 17:535–72.

Kennedy, David M. *Birth Control in America.* New Haven: Yale University Press, 1970.

Lutz, Alma. *Crusade for Freedom—Women of the Antislavery Movement.* Boston: Beacon Press, 1968.

Nall, J. O. *The Tobacco Night Riders of Kentucky and Tennessee, 1905–1909.* Louisville, Ky.: Standard Press, 1942.

Rowan, Richard W. *Secret Agents against America.* New York: Doubleday, Doran, 1939.

Sorin, Gerald. *Abolitionism: A New Perspective.* New York: Praeger, 1972.

Stegner, Wallace. "The Radio Priest and His Flock." Isabell Leighton (ed.), *The Aspirin Age, 1919–1941.* New York: Simon and Schuster, 1949.

Tull, Charles J. *Father Coughlin and the New Deal.* Syracuse, N.Y.: Syracuse University Press, 1965.

Wechsler, James A. *Revolt on the Campus.* New York: Covici, Friede, 1935.

chapter seven

Combat Readiness

"The modern party," Robert Michels wrote more than 50 years ago, "is a fighting organization in the political sense of the term, and must as such conform to the laws of tactics. Now the first article of these laws is facility of mobilization" (1949, p. 41[1]). There is a basic asymmetry in the contest between a challenging group and its antagonist. On the one hand, we have a nascent organization without established member commitment or internal control over members. A challenging group starts with no willing agents at its command; at best, it has sympathizers, some fervent and some easily distracted. It faces organized antagonists who possess all the control over members that established bureaucracies possess. The antagonists typically have available to them full-time professionals who can be deployed and redeployed at the will of the organizational hierarchy.

One way of overcoming the asymmetry is for the challenging group to adopt the organizational pattern of established groups. It can create an apparatus of internal control that enables it to deal on more equal terms with its antagonist. Every challenging group faces the problem that Philip Selznick has addressed in *The Orga-*

---

[1] First published in 1915.

nizational Weapon, "transforming a voluntary association into a managerial structure. . . . Put most simply, the process referred to is one which changes *members* into *agents,* transforms those who merely give consent into those (at an extreme, soldiers) who do work as well as conform" (Selznick, 1960, p. 21).

To fight effectively, a challenging group must solve two related problems that are frequently confounded. The transformation of a voluntary association into a managerial structure involves more than the creation of a high willingness of members to act as agents of the group. Even when challenging groups have a committed membership that can be quickly activated, they may lack unity of command. Competing voices, each with its plausible claim to legitimate authority, are often heard — one saying "March!" another "Wait!" Who speaks for the group? It is not enough to have agents if the problem of who directs these agents is left unresolved. One may convert members into soldiers, but soldiers fight civil wars as well as foreign ones.

Put in somewhat different language, two separate functional problems must be solved for the group to operate effectively in conflict situations. On the one hand, the group must be able to maintain a series of commitments from members that can be activated when necessary — essentially a problem of pattern maintenance. Pattern maintenance exists when the members of a group carry around their membership in latent form even while not actively participating in collective action. When they convene, the individuals are ready to begin functioning immediately as group members again. In this sense, the group continues to exist even while individual members are scattered about and not in direct interaction with each other.

On the other hand, the group must be able to solve problems of internal conflict so that power struggles within the group do not paralyze its ability to act — essentially a problem of integration. Only if both of these functional problems are solved will the group have achieved the necessary combat readiness by marrying the willingness to obey and the right to command.

Of course, all this military language exaggerates. The challenging group remains a voluntary association, and the good soldiers, if they get fed up, desert without facing the firing squad. Claims to authority are not buttressed by any apparatus of legal coercion or by long-established tradition but must be established *de novo.* But the military analogy is a useful one because it alerts us to certain features of the internal organization of challenging groups that are associated with successful outcomes.

BUREAUCRACY

Bureaucratic organization helps a group with the problem of pattern maintenance. By creating a structure of roles with defined expectations in the place of diffuse commitments, a challenging group can better assure that certain necessary tasks will be routinely performed. It gives the challenging group a higher readiness for action.

It is sometimes supposed that challenging groups go through stages, becoming increasingly bureaucratic as they grow older. For the groups in this sample, the reality is considerably more complex. Many groups sprang up as full-blown bureaucracies with more rules and procedures than they had members. Others never assumed the essential characteristics of bureaucratic organizations even after a number of years. Still there is a kernel of truth in the hypothesis of increasing bureaucratization: none of the groups grew less bureaucratic over the years.

Three minimum characteristics are used here to define bureaucratic challenging groups:

1.   The group possesses a written document, a constitution or charter, that states both the purposes of the organization and its provisions for operation. A written document stating only purposes — for example, a manifesto — is insufficient if it contains no provisions for how the group will conduct its business.

2.   The group maintains a formal list of members, thus distinguishing members from mere supporters and sympathizers.

3.   The group possesses three or more levels or internal divisions — for example, officers or executive committee; division, committee, or chapter heads; and rank and file. Groups that have only officers and rank and file do not meet this criterion.

Forty-five percent of the groups (24) met all three criteria of bureaucratic organization at some point during the period of challenge. Are these groups more successful than their more loosely organized counterparts? Figure 7–1 indicates that they are, but only moderately so. The difference is stronger for acceptance (71 percent vs. 28 percent) than for new advantages (62 percent vs. 38 percent). Four of the five co-opted groups, but only two of the six

FIGURE 7-1
Bureaucracy and Outcome

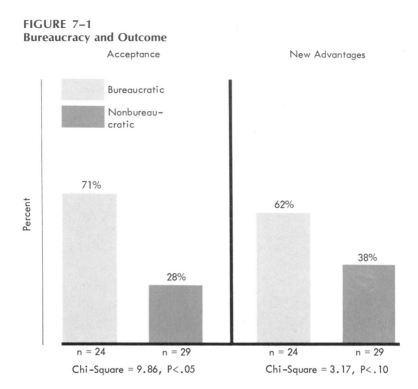

preempted groups are bureaucratic. Apparently imitating the form of one's antagonist eases the development of some sort of working relationship.

It appears also to enhance the group's ability to win new advantages, but here bureaucracy is clearly only part of the story. There are nine bureaucratic groups out of 24 that gain no new advantages in spite of the hypothesized benefits of this form of organization. Why are they unsuccessful?

CENTRALIZATION OF POWER

Our theoretical argument above suggests an answer. Bureaucratic organization aids with the problem of keeping an organization in a state of readiness to act — that is, with the problem of pattern maintenance — but it guarantees nothing with respect to the problem of internal conflict. Now one might well include hierarchy of command in the definition of bureaucratic organization, but it has not been included in the operations used here. Formality of procedures, record keeping, and some complexity of role differentiation are the defining elements, and their relationship to centralization of power remains to be determined.

A challenging group is coded as having a centralized power structure if there is essentially a single center of power within the organization, whether or not this is formally sanctioned. As a matter of fact, the single center of power is frequently associated with personal leadership, with a central figure around whom the organization revolves and with whom it is identified. In some cases, the group is essentially a personal vehicle for such a leader and could hardly be said to exist independently of its core figure.

Slightly over half of the groups (28) have a centralized power structure, and two-thirds of these (19) have a dominant personal leader. The other nine have some form of collective leadership, frequently vested in an executive committee or national board. The executive committee or individual leader may be accountable to the membership and may be responsive to their influence, but we would not code a group as centralized if there were branches or chapters that enjoyed substantial autonomy to act without the formal or informal approval of the center.

Decentralized groups lack such a single center of power. In a few cases, mostly quite small groups, power is diffused through the membership at large. More typically, there are chapters or divisions of the organization that maintain substantial autonomy and the freedom to decide whether or not to support collective action by the group as a whole. Such challenging groups are coalition-like; the elements that make up the group as a whole maintain a separate identity and importance.

Centralization of power, I am suggesting, is the way in which challenging groups deal with the problem of internal conflict and through which they are able to achieve unity of command. Figure 7–2 indicates that, like bureaucracy, centralization of power is also associated with success. Again the relationship is a modest one, but, unlike bureaucracy, it is stronger for gaining new advantages than it is for acceptance. Five of the six preempted groups but only two of the five co-opted groups are centralized.

The argument that bureaucracy and centralization solve two separate functional problems implies that they are making independent contributions to the success of challenging groups. That this is indeed the case can be seen from two pieces of additional evidence. First, there is no relationship between bureaucracy, as measured

FIGURE 7–2
Centralization of Power and Outcome

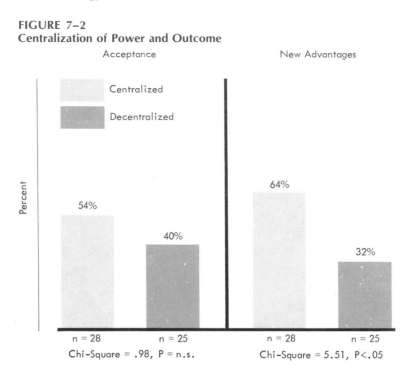

FIGURE 7–3
Bureaucracy and Centralization of Power

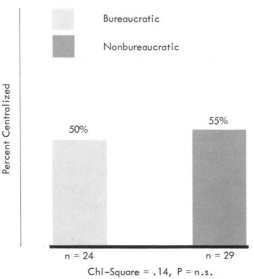

here, and centralization of power. In Figure 7–3, we see that half of the bureaucratic groups had centralized power structures as did approximately half (55 percent) of the nonbureaucratic groups.

That each variable has a modest relationship to success is to be expected if each is solving only one of the problems of combat readiness. Together, the relationship ought to be stronger. Groups that had both bureaucratic structures and centralization of power should have done especially well; those that had neither should have done especially poorly. Figure 7–4 presents these results.

The combination is especially potent with respect to gaining new advantages. Three-fourths of the groups that had both gained new advantages while only 15 percent of those which had neither were successful in this respect. Both variables are relevant for gaining acceptance also, but here bureaucracy is clearly making the

FIGURE 7–4
Bureaucracy and Centralization of Power by Outcome

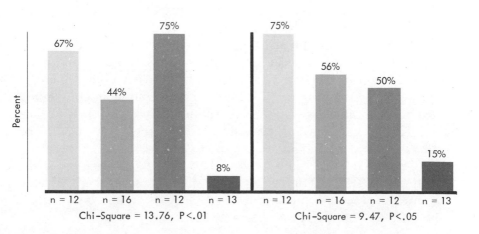

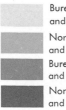

stronger contribution. A group that had neither bureaucratic structure nor centralized power had very little chance of gaining acceptance.

It is worth taking a closer look at some of the deviant cases in Figure 7–4. Two groups, lacking both bureaucracy and centralized power structures, defied the odds against success although only one of these won both acceptance and new advantages. The double-winner was the Federal Suffrage Association. The FSA was but one, and not the most important, carrier of the successful women's suffrage challenge. It began in 1892 and fought for many years but was less prominent than the National American Woman Suffrage Association in the vigorous activity period of 1916 to 1920, preceding the ratification of the constitutional amendment. The group achieved its major objective, but it was neither alone nor always in the center of the struggle. Its organizational strengths or weaknesses may not have been as relevant as for many other groups.

The other exception, the American Free Trade League, was a post-civil war group pursuing tariff reform. They argued that high tariffs placed a heavy burden upon wage earners and farmers and aimed their mobilization efforts at these groups. The League established branches in a number of areas and, with the support of a number of influential newspapers, spread their message throughout the country. During the years of peak activity, they circulated more than half a million of their pamphlets annually. The Free Trade League served as a rallying point for a loose coalition of liberal forces concerned not only with tariff revision but other issues —for example, civil service reform—as well. They were credited with the defeat of a number of protectionist Republican congressmen in the 1870 election. Their new advantages came in the form of small rate reductions in 1870 and 1872, but these were short-lived victories. Although the League was the most active and influential element in the Liberal Republican third-party movement to defeat President Grant in 1872, the Liberal Republican convention went on to nominate a staunch protectionist, Horace Greeley. The Free Trade League went into a state of disarray and ceased to be an active force while Grant was re-elected with ease. It was not long before the limited gains of 1870 and 1872 were removed in the Tariff Act of 1875. The earlier, short-lived successes qualify the League for preemption rather than collapse as an outcome, but its success was both partial and temporary.

There are also exceptions in the opposite direction — groups that had the proper organizational credentials but were unsuccessful. Only two groups that had both centralized power and bureaucratic structures failed to gain at least one form of success although both of them left an important legacy for the future.

The International Workingmen's Association (the First International) was one such group. The I.W.A. was founded in London in 1864 by British trade unionists together with Karl Marx. John Commons suggests that "its starting point was the practical effort of British trade union leaders to organize the workingmen of the continent and to prevent the importation of continental strike-breakers. That Karl Marx wrote its Inaugural Address was merely incidental. It chanced that what he wrote was acceptable to the British unionists. . . . His Inaugural Address was a trade union document, not a Communist Manifesto" (Commons, 1966, p. 205).

The I.W.A. in America was beset by a sharp ideological split from its inception. "The philosophy of the International . . . was based on the economic organization of the working class in trade unions and cooperative societies. These must precede the political seizure of the government by labour. . . . This conception differed widely from the teaching of Ferdinand Lassalle." In Lassallean socialism "there was but one means of solving the labour problem — political action. When political control was finally achieved, the labour party, with the aid of State credit, would build up a network of co-operative societies into which eventually all industry would pass. In short, the distinction between the ideas of the International and of Lassalle consisted in the fact that the former advocated economic organization prior to and underlying political organization, while the latter considered a political victory as the basis of economic organization" (Commons, p. 206).

The International in America reflected this difference; to make matters worse, ideological differences were merged with differences in social background, making the cleavage even sharper and more difficult to manage. The American I.W.A. contained two distinct groups, German wage earners and native American intellectuals. "The most important German forerunner of the International was the General German Workingmen's Union (Der Allegemeine Deutsche Arbeiterverein), which became subsequently known as Section 1 of New York of the International" (Commons, p. 207).

In addition to the immigrants, there was a group of native American radicals who affiliated with the International, with Section 12 becoming the most prominent representative of this group. Section 12 was headed by two sisters, Victoria Woodhull and Tennessee Claflin, "notorious (sic) advocates of woman suffrage and 'social freedom' " (Commons, p. 211).

Now the I.W.A. in America had a Provisional Central Committee dominated by Frederich A. Sorge, the leader of the immigrant sections. Section 12, it appears, was not easy to bring under this central control. Sorge complained repeatedly to the central committee about the activities of the maverick section. "The manifesto signed by William West and published in a certain 'Weekly' in behalf of Section 12 . . . was published and issued *without* the authority or consent of the Central Committee," he wrote. Later, he reported to London, with disapproval, about the activities of Section 12. "The Woodhull-Claflin Section (No. 12) issued a call to the 'citizens of the union' full of empty phraseology. Section 1 protested against it—in vain so far. The right of women to vote and to hold office, the freedom of sexual relations, universal language, pantarchy were preached by Section 12 and slanders were thrown against all opponents" (quoted in Commons, pp. 211–12).

By late 1871, a split between the German immigrant and American elements was imminent. Section 12 was expelled but fought back, organizing the American confederation of the International at a convention in July, 1872, with several other English-speaking sections represented. The split paralleled the Marx-Bakunin split that was rocking the International in Europe at the same time. At the Congress of the Hague in 1872 at which Bakunin was eventually expelled, Bakunists supported the representative of the American intellectuals, William West, while the Marxists supported Sorge.

On returning to New York, Sorge did a rather remarkable job of holding the faction-scarred organization together and active for four more years. During this period, the power centralization lacking earlier was consolidated under Sorge, although internal disharmony remained a problem. The organization never did solve the problem of internal conflict. Perhaps its bureaucratic structure and power centralization enabled it to survive as long as it did, in spite of lack of success and external attack (see the earlier description, p. 77, of its victimization in the so-called Tompkins Square Riot in 1874). Nevertheless, they did not bring it any favorable outcomes.

The other exception, the American Anti-Slavery Society, also suffered from acute factional strife, and, interestingly, the issue of women's rights again played a role. The AASS was dominated by its executive committee in New York under the leadership of Theodore D. Weld, Henry B. Stanton, and James G. Birney. There is historical disagreement about the causes of factionalism in the American Anti-Slavery Society, much of it centering around the historian's view of William Lloyd Garrison. Garrison was the leader of the radical faction within the AASS and confronted the organization with a continuing dilemma. He was given the essentially powerless post of Secretary for Foreign Correspondence, but, even in this apparently innocuous position, he was not trusted to follow the lead of those who controlled the organizational apparatus. "The Executive Committee ordered all letters written by him as Secretary for Foreign Correspondence to be first submitted to the committee for approval. Garrison, chafing at this restraint, resigned the position within a month" (Nye, 1955, p. 73).

But the centralization of power in the American Anti-Slavery Society never really subdued the growing internal differences. As the movement grew in size and importance, the division became increasingly acute. "The struggles that occurred within the AASS before the split at the annual convention in May, 1840 — struggles over the role of women in the movement and over religious and political questions — were . . . manifestations of the more basic radical-conservative conflict" (Kraditor, 1969, p. 10).

Both the International Workingmen's Association and the American Anti-Slavery Society had power centralization and bureaucratic structure without gaining any form of success. They both experienced factional splits. Of the ten successful groups with centralization and bureaucratic structure, only three experienced such factional splits. It is worth looking more closely at this whole issue of factionalism and its relationship to both internal organization and relations with outside groups.

FACTIONALISM

Internal division is a misery that few challenging groups escape completely — it is in the nature of the beast. Men and women of the best intentions, sharing common goals, will disagree on strategy and tactics. They will differ in the priorities they give to different subgoals and in their emphasis on the pursuit of short-range or long-range solutions. And they may compete for control of the organizational apparatus with power as an end in itself, using particular ideological postures as means of gaining support over rivals.

In fact, the content of internal disputes seems to offer very little promise for understanding why factional splits develop and with what effects. There is really no end to the issues that imaginative antagonists can use as a *casus belli*, especially if they happen to be on the political left. "We do not envy the future historian of the American revolutionary movement when he faces the problem of tracing the course of the ephemeral sects," wrote a considerate socialist, "M.S." in *The New International* in December, 1938. He attempts to make the task easier by describing in some detail Trotskyist splinter groups. One such splinter fell into our sample, the Revolutionary Workers League (Revolt), a factional split from a factional split.

The original faction, the "Oehler-Stamm group broke from the then Trotskyist Workers Party around November, 1935, because of chaste opposition to our proposal to enter the Socialist party and unite with its revolutionary wing," writes this spokesmen for the parent group. The group they formed was called the Revolutionary Workers League, but Oehler and Stamm soon had their own falling out. "A furious struggle broke out between Oehler and Stamm," writes M.S.,

> perhaps the greatest dispute since the churchmen gathered for the Council of Nicaea in 325 A.D. to work out what became the Nicene Creed of Catholicism. One faction held that the description of Christ or God the son should read *homo'ousias* or a being of identical substance with God the Father; the other faction held that the Greek word in question properly had another letter, making it read *homoi'ousias* or a being of similar substance with God the Father. Result: the split between the Roman Catholic and the Eastern (Greek Orthodox) churches. Of no less importance was the fight between Oehler and Stamm.

One contended that Trotskyism had degenerated in 1934 while the other claimed that the degeneration had already occurred by 1928. "It seems that Oehler won, after assailing the rebels for their 'false position on democratic centralism [which] has its leader in Stamm, who combines errors of bourgeois democracy with bureaucracy,' to say nothing of his 'ultra-left and false evaluation of Marxism.'" Stamm, however, was not prepared to accept banishment quietly. Not only did he form a rival group, but he chose to call it by the same name, the Revolutionary Workers League, adding still another pitfall for the hapless historian. One small kindness: the new group established its own newspaper, *Revolt,* allowing one to identify them as Revolutionary Workers League (Revolt) to avoid confusion with the Oehler group.

Sometimes, of course, divisions concern more than a single iota. Certainly, to the participants, they seem to involve fundamental differences in principle, however trivial the dispute appears in historical perspective. But given the infinite possibilities of division, it seems more fruitful to approach the issue of factionalism by asking why groups do not split rather than why they do.

The measure of factionalism used here is formal schism. Many challenging groups have vigorous internal opposition, sometimes leading to the expulsion or resignation of individual members. If these disgruntled former members proceed to set up a rival challenging group, the original challenging group is classified as factional; if, like good soldiers, they accept their fate and slowly fade away, the group has escaped factionalism as defined here.

Factional splits were part of the history of 43 percent of the groups in the sample. Sixteen of these experienced splits during their period of challenge; seven others were themselves born of factional disputes — that is, they were created by dissident members of another challenging group as in the case of the Revolutionary Workers League (both versions). Although there might be theoretical arguments for separating these two categories, they are similar empirically and are combined here for convenience of comparison with the 30 groups that experienced no formal schism in their history.

Figure 7-5 indicates that the sorry reputation of factionalism is a deserved one. It is especially related to the achievement of new advantages; less than one-fourth of the groups that experience it are successful, in contrast to 70 percent of those that escape it. For reasons that will become clearer when we examine the relationship between factionalism, bureaucracy, and power centralization, it is less sharply related to gaining acceptance.

Factional splits, I am arguing, are the primary manifestation of the failure of the group to solve the problem of internal conflict. All groups experience internal disagreement but only some divide. That factional splits are a concomitant of failure is clear enough, but the causal status of factionalism is far from clear. It is possible that it makes an important contribution to failure. No one would

FIGURE 7–5
Factionalism and Outcome

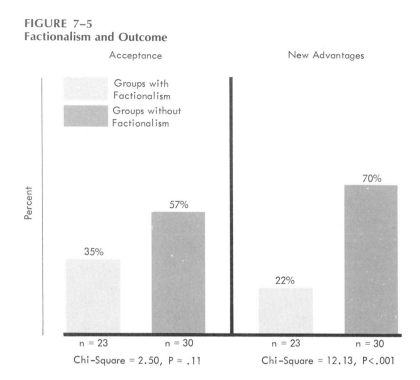

suggest that a group, well-launched on the road to success, is suddenly and capriciously struck down by this malady, but a strong argument can be made that it is an essential link in a chain of events that leads to failure. In this view, groups that lack mechanisms for dealing with internal division become crippled by factionalism and succumb when they might have succeeded.

An alternative line of argument minimizes the importance of factionalism, viewing it primarily as an epiphenomenon. In this view, factionalism is merely a manifestation of failure and not a cause. It develops in moribund groups, and, while it may hasten their collapse, it helps very little in understanding the dynamics of success or failure.

A reasonable guess is that there is some degree of two-way causality between factionalism and failure. Groups that are not doing well are prone to defection by dissident leaders with their own following. The exit of part of the group deprives it of a major source of energy and skill that might have allowed it either to persevere until its strategy bore results or to correct its course to a more successful one (cf. Hirschman, 1970).

But to acknowledge mutual influence does not imply that it is equal in both directions. By examining the sources and consequences of factional splits, we can gain some purchase on the issue of causality.

STIMULATING AND CONTAINING FACTIONALISM

I have argued that natural heterogeneity provides sufficient cause for a factional split if a group lacks adequate mechanisms for managing internal conflict. But perhaps these internal differences are helped along by hostile outsiders. Gary Marx (1972) discusses a series of documented cases of the use of agents provocateur in contemporary challenging groups. Many had the explicit purpose of promoting discord and distrust. The FBI has subsequently admitted a systematic program aimed at disrupting militant black and leftist groups. Political sabotage of the sort so extensively revealed during the Watergate scandal frequently had a similar objective.

Conceivably, such shadowy figures were present among some of the challenging groups in this historical sample, but there is no evidence of anyone later revealed as an agent of outside groups playing a role in any of the splits that occurred. Unfortunately, we can never be certain that such dirty tricks were absent, but there is no positive evidence suggesting it.

Open attacks on the group by its enemies can be evaluated more easily. In particular, we can ask if factional splits were usually preceded by external attacks upon the group, implying that it broke up under outside pressure. In contrast, we can speculate that internal division advertises weakness and invites attack by antagonists looking for a safe opportunity; thus attacks might tend to follow rather than precede a factional split.

By external attack, I mean the application of violence, arrest or other constraints to group members by outsiders. Of the 23 groups with factionalism, 17 experienced no attack either in the two years before or the two years after a factional split.[2] The other six did experience attack, half before the factional split and half afterwards. In other words, only three of the 23 groups experienced factionalism following attacks, and, even in these three cases, there is ample evidence of sharp internal divisions before the attack. If ex-

---

[2] For groups that were born of a factional split, this refers to attacks on the predecessor from whom they issued.

ternal pressure hastened the ultimate disintegration in these cases, this still occurred in less than 15 percent of the groups.

In general, then, challenging groups seem to contain the seeds of internal division within themselves. They find ample basis for fratricide in the natural frictions of cohabiting a common cause, independently of any contribution from those outsiders who would encourage their disharmony. The critical question remains, not why internal division arises, but how it is contained and managed. What mechanisms help a group to keep internal divisions from resulting in formal schism?

If we are correct in arguing that centralization of power is a device for managing internal division, then we ought to find that it is related to factionalism. Figure 7–6 indicates a substantial relationship: only 25 percent of the groups with centralization of power experienced factional splits, while this was the lot of almost two-thirds of the decentralized groups.

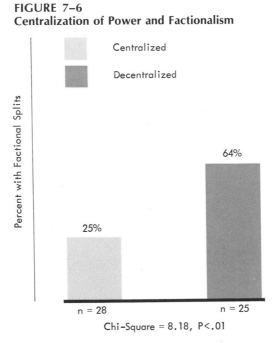

FIGURE 7–6
Centralization of Power and Factionalism

There is some suggestive evidence that factionalism is connected with failure independently of its connection with decentralization. Decentralized groups are not only more likely to develop factional splits to begin with but are *more likely to be hurt by them if they de-velop.* Of the 25 decentralized groups, 16 developed factional splits. As Figure 7–7 shows, only one-eighth of those which developed factionalism were able to gain new advantages, but two-thirds of these decentralized groups that somehow escaped factionalism were successful in winning new advantages. Decentralized groups, then, have a reduced ability to avoid factional splits, but, if they are able somehow to manage their internal differences, they do quite well in spite of their lack of centralized power. One reason that they do well is that they have another organizational attribute that promotes success — bureaucratic organization. Only eight decentralized groups were able to win new advantages, but six of these were bureaucratic.

FIGURE 7–7
Factionalism and Outcome for Decentralized Groups

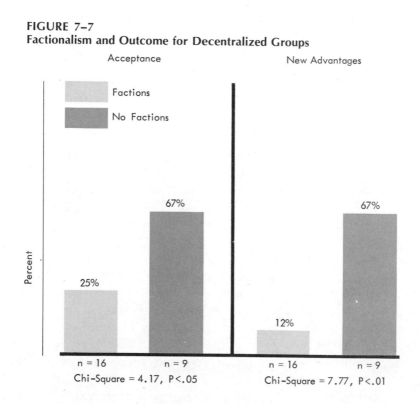

Bureaucracy has its effect on success independently of factionalism. One can make a plausible theoretical case that bureaucracy either helps to control factional splits or encourages them. A group that subjects members to tight organizational discipline ought to be able to suppress dissent and thus avoid factionalism, but Zald and Ash (1966) make exactly the opposite argument, relying on a distinction between "inclusive and exclusive" organization.

> The inclusive organization requires minimum levels of initial commitment — a pledge of general support without specific duties, a short indoctrination period or none at all. On the other hand, the exclusive organization is likely to hold the new recruit in a long "novitiate" period, to require the recruit to subject himself to organization discipline and orders. . . . Inclusive and exclusive challenging groups differ not only in recruitment procedures and requirements, but they also differ in the amount of participation required. The inclusive [group] typically requires little activity from its members — they can belong to other organizations and groups unselfconsciously, and their behavior is not as permeated by organization goals, policies, and tactics. On the other hand, the exclusive organization not only requires that a greater amount of energy and time be spent in movement affairs, but it more extensively permeates all sections of the members' life, including activities with non-members (Zald and Ash, pp. 330–331).

In spite of the greater ability of exclusive organizations to make demands on members, Zald and Ash suggest that it will be more faction prone. "The inclusive organization with its looser criteria of affiliation and of doctrinal orthodoxy is more split-resistant than the exclusive organization. The inclusive organization retains its factions while the exclusive organization spews them forth" (p. 337).

The vast majority of challenging groups in this study are inclusive organizations by almost any criterion. The one used here to define exclusiveness is the presence of a probationary period or investigation after which a would-be member is formally inducted.

Only five groups in the sample meet this minimal measure of exclusiveness, but they were neither more nor less likely to experience factionalism than their inclusive counterparts. Two of the five had factional splits while 44 percent of the inclusive groups did also. Another two of the five also gained new advantages — but these were groups that managed to escape factionalism.

The Zald-Ash hypothesis remains a suggestive one and does not deserve to be dismissed on the evidence of five cases. But the result is consistent with our explanation that individual member commitment — an issue of pattern maintenance — tells us little about the ability of the group to handle internal conflict.

Further evidence on this is provided by the absence of any substantial relationship between bureaucratic organization and factionalism. In Figure 7–8, 50 percent of the bureaucratic organizations experienced factional splits, but only 38 percent of the nonbureaucratic groups had this malady. If anything, bureaucracy is associated with more rather than less factionalism. Bureaucracy and factionalism are independently associated with outcome. When bureaucratic groups avoid factional splits, 83 percent win new advantages (10 of 12); when they experience factional splits, only 42 percent are successful in this regard (5 of 12). Put another way, groups that succeed in spite of factional splits are bureaucratic. Only five groups with factionalism won new advantages but all were bureaucratic; eight factional groups won acceptance and all but one was bureaucratic.

FIGURE 7–8
Bureaucracy and Factionalism

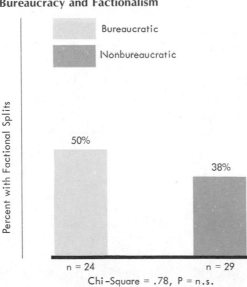

Bureaucratic

Nonbureaucratic

Percent with Factional Splits

50%

38%

n = 24   n = 29

Chi-Square = .78, P = n.s.

SUMMARY

Challenging groups are involved in political conflict. They are ready for such combat if they maintain a structure of specific commitment on the part of members that enables them to conduct routine tasks between battles so that they are ready for action when necessary. Bureaucratic organization provides a solution to the first problem of combat readiness — a cadre of reliable workers with coordinated tasks. Its contribution to the management of internal dissent is minimal; bureaucratic groups are at least as likely to experience factional splits as nonbureaucratic ones. But their ability to act quickly also depends on their having solved the problem of internal division. Centralization of power is an organizational device for handling the problem of internal division and providing unity of command. It has much to do with preventing factionalism, but sometimes (25 percent of the time), such centralized groups experience factional splits anyway. Furthermore, decentralized groups are able to escape factionalism in a substantial minority of cases.

Each of these variables — bureaucracy, centralization of power, and factionalism — makes a contribution to success, and there is a substantial interaction between centralization and factionalism. A centralized, bureaucratic group that escapes factional splits is highly likely to be successful; so, in fact, is a decentralized, bureaucratic group that escapes factionalism, but it is less likely to escape than its centralized counterpart.

A decentralized, nonbureaucratic group that experiences factionalism is doomed to failure; but, if it somehow manages to escape factionalism, it still has a modest possibility of success. Its chances of escaping a split are considerably enhanced if it has a centralized power structure. There are, then, definite advantages for a challenging group, inevitably engaged in conflict with an organized antagonist, to organize itself for facility in political combat.

REFERENCES

Commons, John R., et al., *History of Labor in the United States*, Vol. II. New York: A. M. Kelley, 1966.

Hirschman, Albert O. *Exit, Voice, and Loyalty*. Cambridge, Mass.: Harvard University Press, 1970.

Kraditor, Aileen S. *Means and Ends in American Abolitionism*. New York: Pantheon Books, 1969.

Marx, Gary T. "Thoughts on a Neglected Category of Social Movement Participant: The Agent Provocateur and Informant." Paper delivered at the American Sociological Association meetings, New Orleans, 1972.

Michels, Robert. *Political Parties*. Glencoe, Ill.: Free Press, 1949.

Nye, Russell B. *William Lloyd Garrison and the Humanitarian Reformers*. Boston: Little, Brown, 1955.

Selznick, Philip. *The Organizational Weapon*. Glencoe, Ill.: Free Press, 1960.

Zald, Mayer N. and Ash, Roberta. "Social Movement Organizations; Growth, Decay, and Change." *Social Forces,* March, 1966, 44:327–41.

chapter eight

The Historical Context of Challenges

The United States has changed immensely from that summer day in 1816 when the North Carolina Manumission Society held its first general meeting to the winter day in 1941 when A. Philip Randolph proposed that 10,000 black people march on Washington to demand an end to racial discrimination in defense employment. We have treated all 53 challenging groups as part of the same society, but the predominantly rural, pre-industrial America of the early 19th century can hardly be considered the same society as the urban, industrial giant poised on the edge of World War II.

There is no research method without its costs. In searching for patterns in the careers of a sample of diverse challenging groups, we have ripped each from its historical context. Each challenge has a thousand unique features that have been studiously ignored. It would be an idle conceit to pretend that this chapter will somehow rectify past neglect. My intention at this point is not to restore the challenging groups to their special setting but to render the setting itself amenable to the same type of generalization that earlier chapters have pursued.

Three related questions about historical context will concern us:
    1.   Are certain kinds of historical periods especially profitable

for launching challenges? For example, are turbulent or quiet periods more conducive to success? How does a major crisis such as war or economic collapse affect the chances of a challenging group succeeding?

2.   Have there been significant shifts in what it takes for a challenging group to succeed in the 125 years between the first and last challenger in the sample? More specifically, did groups find it easier or more difficult to mount successful challenges in an earlier age? Have their strategies and characteristics changed over the years? Did they become more or less bureaucratic and centralized? Were violence and other constraints more or less frequent in earlier periods? What long term trends exist, if any?

3.   Do the relationships discovered earlier hold generally or only for certain historical periods? More specifically, does success have the same connection with challenging group goals, strategy, and organization at different times?

CRISIS AND SUCCESS

In quiet times, a challenging group faces a political system well-equipped to deal with would-be troublemakers. There is reserve capacity or slack resources that can be mobilized to control a challenging group if necessary. In system-wide crisis periods, this state of affairs no longer holds because there is little slack that can be diverted for social control purposes.

This is true for both external or internal crises. In an external crisis — for example, a foreign war or natural disaster — the ability of the system to achieve collective goals is on trial. It is a crisis precisely because the reserve capacity of the political system must be employed to deal with the problem and its effects. In quiet times, it may be cheaper to devote resources to controlling a demanding challenging group rather than giving it what it wants, but this balance is shifted in crisis. It frequently becomes more convenient to yield than to divert precious resources from an already strained system for purposes of social control.

Internal crises produce the same effect. As with external crises, the reserve capacity is employed, in this case to deal not only with the conditions of crisis but also with the many challengers pressing their demands simultaneously. Resources are not available to control all of the challengers at once, and it becomes more convenient to come to terms with some of them. This argument, then, suggests a hypothesis: challenging groups should enjoy relatively greater success in times of general crisis than in quiet times.

Are challenges initiated during times of crisis more successful than those launched in quiet times? With respect to wars, the question is moot: none of our 53 challenging groups began during a major war.[1] This is not surprising. As Ash (1972, p. 179) observes, "A national war effort can be understood as a movement phenomenon . . . in which an elite mobilizes a large portion of the population, exciting them ideologically and deroutinizing them." When the government enters the mobilization arena in a major way, it is difficult for any mere challenging group to compete successfully for the same constituency; in any event, no group in our sample initiated a challenge in these circumstances.

We can, however, compare challenges launched in periods of social unrest with those started in quiet times. Almost three-fourths of the groups (39) began during relatively turbulent periods, periods characterized by major social movements and many new and diversified challenges. In particular, the 1830s, the period from 1880 until the eve of World War I (including the populist and progressive eras), and the 1930s are treated here as turbulent times. Any challenging group beginning during these periods had very substantial competition for center stage. The effect of the competition, I have hypothesized, is to benefit all by making it more difficult to control any.

Figure 8–1 indicates no support for this hypothesis. The 14 challenging groups that began their challenge in quiet times with relatively little competition do neither better nor worse than their brethren in turbulent times. One gets a similar result in looking at a more direct measure of competition. About three-fifths (30) of the challenging groups were operating in a situation in which another group existed at the same time, attempting to appeal to the same constituency. Again it can be argued that multiple challengers, especially when they offer a division of labor between more radical and moderate alternatives, enhance each other's effectiveness. Or more precisely, the existence of a radical challenger in the field helps the cause of the more moderate challenger.

---

[1] That is, the Civil War, World War I, or World War II. The Mexican War, the Spanish-American War, and the various Indian wars could not really be considered general crisis occasions. The War of 1812 might be considered major, but the first challenging group in the sample emerged in 1816.

FIGURE 8–1
Turbulent Times and Outcome

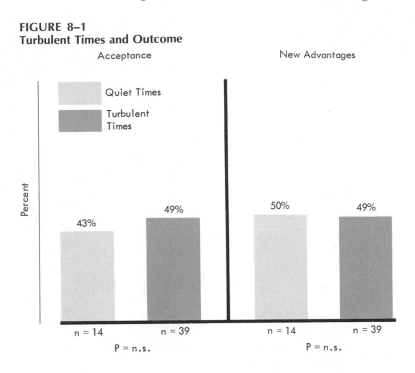

I am unable to discover any evidence that such competition makes a difference. Overall, as Figure 8–2 shows, having a competitor has no effect on success. Figure 8–3 subdivides the competitive groups into three parts: those with a more moderate competitor (10 groups), those with a more radical competitor (7 groups), and those with no consistent difference from their major competitor in militancy of tactics or goals (13 groups). Included in this last category are, for example, unions engaged in jurisdictional disputes with rivals or any group that claims its rival is less effective on grounds unrelated to degree of militancy or radicalness. Again, little or no difference is revealed in Figure 8–3. There is a suggestion that having a radical competitor makes it easier for a group to win acceptance than having a moderate competitor, but the differences with respect to new advantages are negligible.

It is obvious that if the rate of success is the same in turbulent and quiet periods, a larger number of groups will be winning new advantages and success when many are making challenges. But we have found no evidence that these turbulent periods are associated

FIGURE 8–2
Competition and Outcome

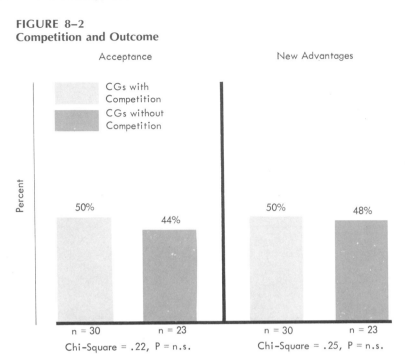

with relative success. However, before abandoning the quest for a relationship completely, there is an additional, more subtle argument to consider.

In this argument, crisis is an aid to those challengers who have already launched their effort and have sustained it, although without results, up to the time of the crisis. Such challenges are not part of the crisis itself and are seen as merely a distraction from the effort needed to manage the immediate more general challenge. The result is that challenging groups will be under pressure to postpone their demands in exchange for the promise of future advantage, and antagonists will be pressed to normalize their relationships with the challenging group. In war, for example, the national effort is provided as justification for sacrifices by both management and labor. Unions are asked to postpone wage demands and avoid strikes for higher wages, management to extend recognition to unions—all in the interest of industrial stability for war production.

This process is not as clear for groups that launch their challenge during the crisis. They are pressing new demands at a time when the system is having trouble meeting existing ones. They may be seen as aggravating an already strained situation and having picked an especially unpropitious time to initiate a challenge. That we find no new challenges launched during wars is consistent with this argument — would-be challengers find it impossible to even surface, let alone succeed. Implicit in this argument is a view of an important third-party or audience role (cf. Schattschneider, 1960 and Lipsky, 1970). The challenging group and antagonist are pressured to make peace — the one by accepting a promissory note for future delivery, the other by giving such a promissory note with acceptance, and a continuing relationship implied.

To explore this argument, we will make two comparisons, one focusing on the role of major wars and the other on the Great Depression. About two-fifths (22) of the groups had challenges in progress when the country became involved in a major war. One of these, the United Sons of Vulcan, started in 1858 and spanned the Civil War, 14 more spanned World War I, and another seven lasted into World War II. The remaining 31 groups carried out their challenge entirely in peacetime.

FIGURE 8-3
Nature of Competitor and Outcome

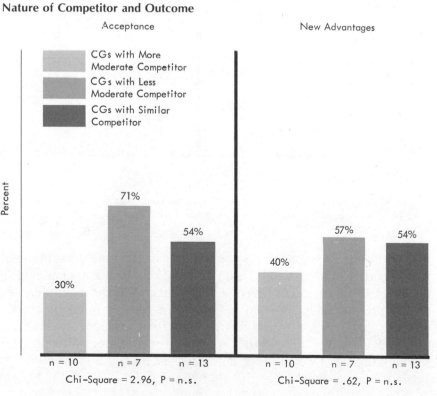

Figure 8–4 shows that there is a greater success for challenging groups when a war occurs during their challenge period. This is especially true for acceptance, where 77 percent during wartime are successful while only about one-quarter of the all peacetime challengers gain acceptance. The result is less dramatic with respect to winning new advantages (64 percent vs. 39 percent) but still suggestive.

FIGURE 8–4
Wars and Outcome

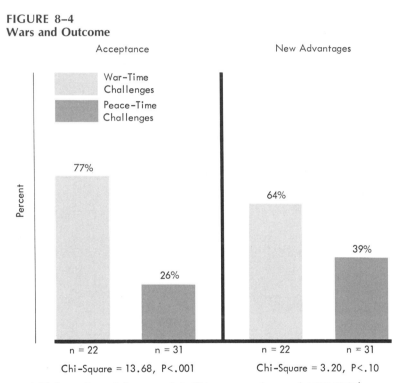

* Challenges begun before a war but still in progress when a major war started.
† Challenges begun and settled during peacetime periods.

The difference between new advantages and gaining acceptance suggests that co-optation is a wartime danger for challenging groups. War occurred during the period of challenge in only one of the six preempted groups but in four of the five co-opted groups. It appears that, at least with a few groups, the pressure to normalize relations with the antagonist produces acceptance, but the deferred concessions are never delivered, at least not within the 15 years following the end of the challenge.

In Figure 8–5, we focus on the effect of the Great Depression. Here we can directly compare those groups that launched a challenge prior to the depression — a challenge that was still unresolved when the depression came — with those who began their challenge while the country was in the throes of this national crisis. The nine pre-depression groups are markedly more successful, this time especially with respect to gaining new advantages. While only 30 percent of the depression-born groups were eventually successful in gaining new advantages, 89 percent of the pre-depression groups achieved this form of success eventually.

Before we can conclude that crisis gives a boost to groups that started their challenge earlier, we must consider an important contaminating variable — having target-displacement goals. As we will see shortly, the results in Figure 8–5 (concerning the depression) turn out to be largely spurious, but the results in Figure 8–4 (concerning war) hold up under this control. One of the effects of the

FIGURE 8–5
The Great Depression and Outcome

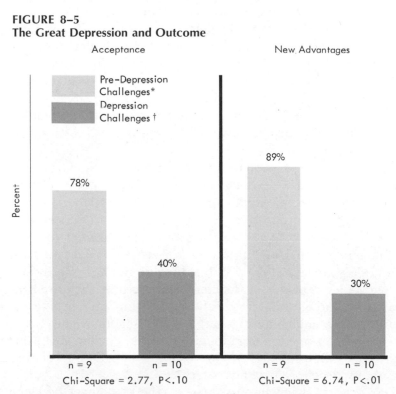

* Challenges initiated before 1929 but still in progress when the depression occurred.
† Challenges begun from 1929 to 1940.

depression was to stimulate challenging groups with goals of replacing their antagonist; in fact, six of the ten depression-spawned groups were of this type. In contrast, none of the nine pre-depression groups had such goals. Several of them (five of nine) were unions that had been struggling for many years and were finally able to consolidate their position under New Deal legislation and support.

Those groups born during the depression that did not attempt to displace their antagonist were as successful as their pre-depression counterparts. All four of these challengers won acceptance, and three of the four gained new advantages also. The three double-successes were all militant unions—Harry Bridges' West Coast Longshoremen, and the CIO-backed Steel Workers Organizing Committee, and Packinghouse Workers Organizing Committee. Although launched in the depression, it took World War II to provide the needed boost for these three challengers. Controlling for target-displacement goals does not eliminate the effect of war on success. In Figure 8-6, we repeat Figure 8-4 only for those groups that do not have target-displacement goals. If anything, the effects of war are sharpened rather than diminished. Only one of 18 wartime challengers fails to gain acceptance while less than one-third of all peacetime challengers gain this form of success. As in the figure for all groups, the differences are much smaller for gaining new advantages, indicating again that co-optation is much more likely to be an outcome for wartime groups than for their peacetime counterparts.

The hypothesized mechanism for success is third-party pressure on the antagonist. Although antagonists have not accepted the challenging group, its ability to survive has convinced many bystanders that the group is a permanent fixture. In noncrisis times, these third parties do not become involved in what they see as someone else's quarrel, but in times of crisis it is everyone's quarrel and they are less tolerant. While they do not necessarily support the particular demands of the challenging group, they are likely to be a strong force for institutionalizing the conflict. This means that they pressure antagonists to bargain and negotiate and, hence, to extend implicit or explicit recognition to the challenging group. In many cases, but not always, the resultant negotiating relationship eventually produces new advantages.

This process is nicely illustrated by the settlement between the Steel Workers Organizing Committee (SWOC) and its most bitter antagonist, the Little Steel companies. "What happens to labor-management relations when a war starts?" David McDonald of the United States Steelworkers asks (1969, p. 152). "Usually, they're frozen, and in the case of the steel industry in the United States in December, 1941, that wasn't a very satisfactory state of affairs. We were in the midst of our first negotiations with Little Steel. Nothing had yet been resolved and — for the moment, at least — it appeared nothing would be. . . . President Roosevelt immediately called upon organized labor and business to forget their differences and unite to provide the material needed to prosecute the war."

FIGURE 8–6
Wars and Outcome for Nontarget-Displacement Groups Only

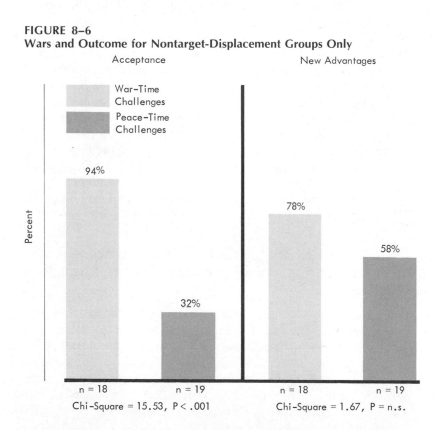

Eventually, President Roosevelt created the National War Labor Board to mediate whatever disputes might arise. The dead-locked Little Steel negotiations were taken to this board and the NWLB issued its famous "Little Steel Formula" in July, 1942, providing a 5½ cent cost-of-living increase in pay, checkoff of union dues, and a maintenance of membership provision that required every man signed up by the union to continue his membership and dues checkoff during the life of the agreement. Nobody was satisfied. The companies didn't like the union security provisions and the union felt the pay raise was totally inadequate. [Philip] Murray called a meeting of the SWOC district representatives and explained the decision to them, making no specific recommendation as to whether or not they should approve it. They were confused and undecided and, while they debated among themselves, R. J. Thomas, president of the United Automobile Workers and a member of the NWLB, cornered Murray and me. He had been listening to the proceedings as an invited guest.

He shifted a massive chew of tobacco from one side of his mouth to the other as he told us: "You fellows don't seem to understand that you got something a lot more important than wages. You got the union security you wanted and the checkoff. These things will really make your union grow. What the hell else do you want?"

On impulse, Murray introduced Thomas to the delegates and he told them what he had just told us. Murray then repeated his denouncement of the wage provisions but stressed the importance of union security. I spoke last, taking the position that the advantages of the security provisions more than offset the disappointing wage scale, and moving that the NWLB recommendations be accepted. They were, and at last we had moved permanently into the ranks of Little Steel (McDonald, pp. 153–54).

If the union had doubts, the Little Steel companies were unambivalently negative toward the Little Steel Formula. The president of Bethlehem Steel

characterized the decision as one which ignored "the basic principles upon which our government was founded and the result . . . will be harmful to our national economy and to the war effort." A statement by the president of Republic Steel said in part: "In *normal times* the company would exercise its right to appeal to the courts to test the legality of [the] directive orders [emphasis added]." Frank Purness of Youngstown Sheet and Tube also characterized the WLB decisions as contrary to the national interest but indicated acquiescence for patriotic reasons (Galenson, 1960, p. 118).

Tom Girdler, the leader of the Little Steel opposition to the Steel Workers Organizing Committee, gave the clearest indication that industry acceptance resulted only from external pressure by the government. "In our private discussions, my associates and I find ourselves unreconciled. We can't help but feel that if the checkoff, which is now a fact in the steel industry, had been resisted by business generally as effectively as we and our employees resisted it in that so-called strike in Little Steel, everybody in the country would have been the gainer" (quoted in Galenson, p. 119).

Wartime challengers are, in many cases, long-time challengers. They manage to stay alive and active in spite of not having stabilized their relationship with their antagonists, and when a war or other system-wide crisis finally comes along, they are able to cash in. Sixteen groups had a challenge period lasting longer than 20 years, and all but three of these were eventually successful. These long-timers had some interesting characteristics. They were, as Figure 8–7 shows, more bureaucratic than the others (75 percent vs. 29 percent), but, if anything, they had less power centralization (44 percent vs. 58 percent).

Figure 8–7 helps to explain an earlier result. We noted in Chapter Seven (see p. 93) that bureaucracy had a stronger re-

FIGURE 8–7
Length of Challenge by Bureaucracy and Power Centralization

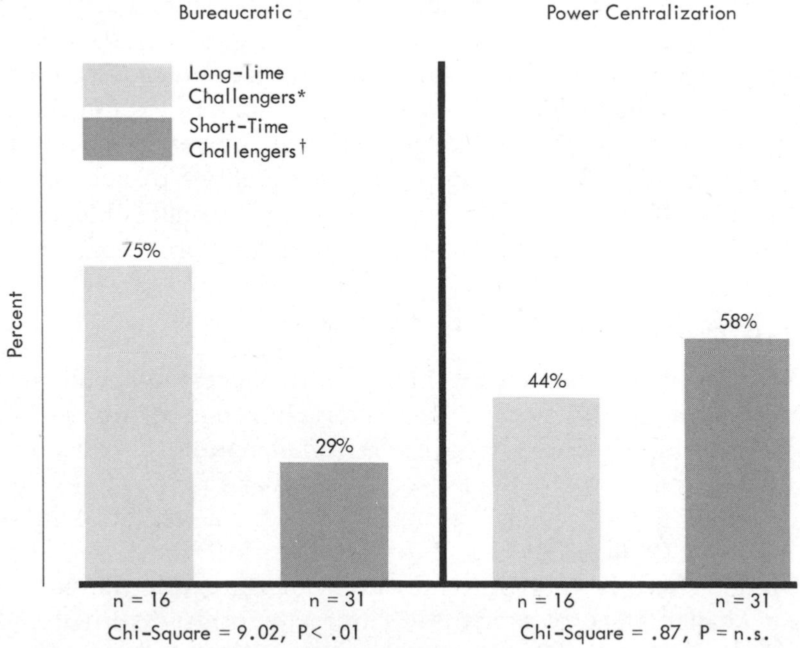

	Bureaucratic	Power Centralization

Long-Time Challengers*
Short-Time Challengers†

75%
29%
44%
58%

n = 16   n = 31   n = 16   n = 31
Chi-Square = 9.02, P< .01   Chi-Square = .87, P = n.s.

* These groups had a period of challenge lasting 20 years or more.
† These groups had a period of challenge of less than 10 years.

lationship to one measure of success—acceptance—while centralization was more strongly related to the other—new advantages. Now we note that long-term challengers tend to be more bureaucratic than short-timers but not more centralized and, further, that groups with a challenge in progress when a crisis arrives have a clear advantage in winning acceptance but a more equivocal one in gaining new advantages. Putting these results together suggests that third-party pressure in a crisis may be a mechanism that connects bureaucracy and acceptance. Bureaucracy helps a group to survive for a longer period in the absence of tangible results; a system-wide crisis then occurs and outside pressures push the group's antagonist to make some accommodation with it. The result is a higher rate of acceptance for bureaucratic groups.

Long-time challengers were also much less likely to seek to displace their antagonist. In fact, only one of the 16 groups that sought to replace its antagonist managed to remain active for over 20 years but without gaining success. This group, the venerable Young People's Socialist League (YPSL) began in 1915 and still surfaces from time to time in one or another incarnation.

In summary, a crisis seems to help only certain kinds of challenging groups. If a group does not aim to displace its antagonist, and if it organizes itself so that it is able to survive and persist, it is in a position to benefit by outside pressures on its antagonist in a national crisis. Being handy, the group is available to exploit the opportunity provided. Its immediate reward, however, is not the ripened fruit of new advantages but the seedlings of acceptance. Eventually, when the crisis is past, the group is usually able to reap a satisfactory harvest, but sometimes the plants prove barren.

TRENDS IN OUTCOME

What long term trends are there in the success of challenging groups? Eight "early" groups began their challenge before the Civil War; 27 "middle" groups began their challenge in the period between the Civil War and the eve of World War I (1865–1913); and the remaining 18 "recent" groups began their challenge in the period from 1914 to the U.S. entry into World War II.

Overall, there is very little indication of change in the success rate of challenging groups in these different periods. As Figure 8–8 shows, there is no difference in the rate of acceptance between middle and recent groups—about half of each are successful in this regard. The early groups had more difficulty with acceptance — only 25 percent were successful.

There might appear to be some modest difference with respect to gaining new advantages, but this result is completely accounted for by the higher frequency of groups with target-displacement goals in recent times. The depression, in particular, bred a large percentage of these groups, and, when one compares only the other kind, there is no advantage for the middle groups over the more recent ones. More precisely, 70 percent of the recent groups and 75 percent of the middle groups gain new advantages when we consider only those without target-displacement goals.

Incidentally, preemption as an outcome does not appear among recent groups; none of the six preempted groups began a challenge after 1914. Co-optation, in contrast, is a more modern phenomenon; none of the five co-opted groups began its challenge before

FIGURE 8–8
Trends in Outcome

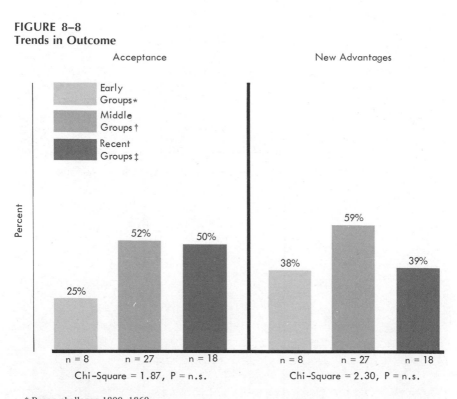

* Began challenge 1800–1860.
† Began challenge 1865–1913.
‡ Began challenge 1914–1945.

1880, and this outcome extends to some recent groups. But this is an isolated strand of evidence based on a handful of cases. We must leave this potential will-o-the-wisp as a lure for some future scholar.

Figure 8–9 explores trends in other characteristics of these groups. One might have expected recent groups to be more bureaucratized, but, if anything, they were less so. Only one-third of the post-1914 groups had bureaucratic structures compared to more than half of the remainder. With power centralization, there is no

FIGURE 8–9
Trends in Characteristics of Challenging Groups

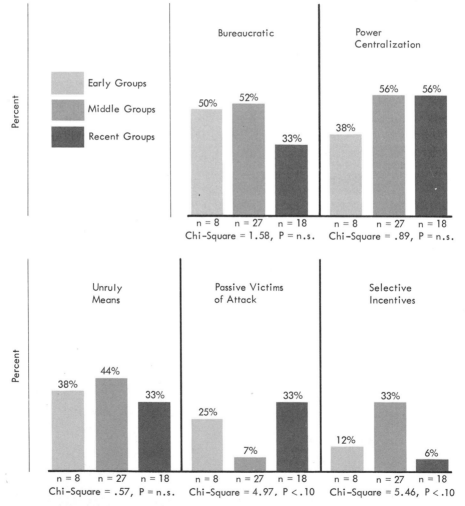

trend at all except for slightly less concentration among the eight pre-civil war groups.

Nor are recent groups more unruly in means than middle and early groups. Only one-third of the post-1914 challengers made use of violence, strikes, or other constraints as a means of influence while a slightly higher percentage of the remainder (43 percent) utilized such means.

But while challenging groups have not become more unruly, their enemies may have. In Chapter Six, we noted the low success rate of groups that use no constraints but are subjected to violent attack or arrest of leaders and members. Only two of 27 middle groups (7 percent) but one-third of the recent groups were the passive victims of such measures.

These victimized groups in the recent period were, with one exception, target-displacement groups. While in earlier periods, some of the groups were victimized primarily by mobs of hostile private citizens or privately hired "detectives" and security forces, all of the recent victims were subjected to arrest by governmental authorities.

Figure 8-9 also shows a decline from middle groups to recent groups in the percent that make use of selective incentives. One-third of the middle groups used such incentives to supplement ideological appeals, but only one recent group among 18 (6 percent) employed this means of mobilization.

The trend that emerges here is a slight increase in groups of the following type: they sought the displacement of their antagonist, with some advocating violence to achieve this goal, but none ever got around to using it; they relied on ideological appeals without supplementing them with selective incentives for individual members; they lacked an organizational structure that produces combat readiness; and they were subjected to arrest and other constraints by hostile authorities. It is not a formula that makes a challenger prosper in American society.

HISTORICAL CONTEXT CONTROLLED

In earlier sections of this chapter, we have explored the relevance of particular historical contexts for the outcome of challenges and the extent to which challenging groups have changed through the years. In this final section, our concern is with the historical period as a limit on the validity of the relationships reported earlier. We found success to be related to certain strategies of mobilization and influence and to certain characteristics of goals and internal organization. But perhaps these relationships were only true during certain periods and not generally. Power central-ization, for example, was found to have some relationship to suc-cess. Is the relationship as true in recent times as in earlier days?

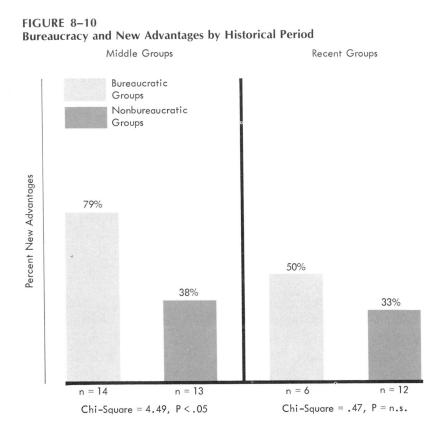

FIGURE 8–10
Bureaucracy and New Advantages by Historical Period

Middle Groups   Recent Groups

Bureaucratic Groups

Nonbureaucratic Groups

Percent New Advantages

79%

38%

50%

33%

n = 14   n = 13   n = 6   n = 12
Chi-Square = 4.49, P < .05   Chi-Square = .47, P = n.s.

We are handicapped in answering this question by the small number of cases. First, we must ignore the eight early groups since once we begin subdividing them into bureaucratic vs. non-bureaucratic and the like, the numbers are too small for any mean-ingful comparison of success rates. Hence, we will only contrast the 27 middle groups with the 18 recent ones. Second, we cannot control for time period unless the variable in question is distributed in reasonable quantity over both middle and recent periods. This limits our focus to the first three variables in Figure 8–9: bureaucratic structure, power centralization, and the use of constraints. Finally, to simplify presentation, we will focus on the relationship of these variables to new advantages rather than using both outcome measures.

FIGURE 8–11
Centralization of Power and New Advantages by Historical Period

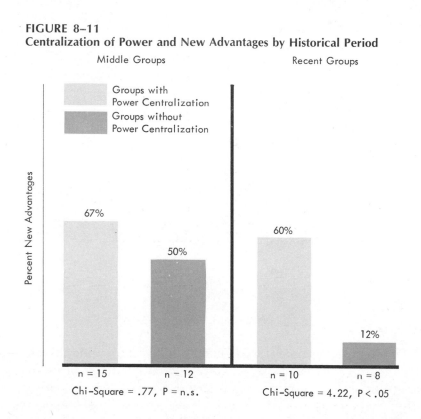

Middle Groups   Recent Groups

Groups with Power Centralization
Groups without Power Centralization

Percent New Advantages

67%
50%
60%
12%

n = 15   n − 12   n = 10   n = 8
Chi–Square = .77, P = n.s.   Chi–Square = 4.22, P < .05

Figures 8–10 to 8–12 compare the relationship of the three variables above with success for middle and recent groups. Basically, the direction of the relationships found earlier hold for both historical periods. Groups that were bureaucratized, that had centralized power structures, and used constraints were more successful than nonbureaucratized, noncentralized, nonconstraint users in both historical eras. One suggestive difference emerges: bureaucratic organization is more sharply related to success than is power centralization for middle groups, but this order is reversed for recent groups.

128   *The Strategy of Social Protest*

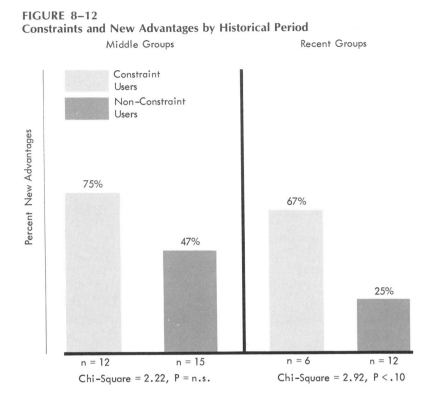

FIGURE 8–12
Constraints and New Advantages by Historical Period

SUMMARY

The historical context adds something to our understanding of the dynamics of success and failure of challenging groups but does not force us to reconsider any earlier conclusions. Having many other challenging groups in the field at the same time does not seem to have much effect on the probability of success of any given challenger. However, a major crisis such as war or economic collapse can aid those challengers who have established their presence before the crisis occurs. A group that is not attempting to displace its antagonists and has organized itself for a long battle is in a position to exploit the opportunity presented by a crisis.

The internal organization of challenging groups has not changed greatly over the years, but there is a tendency in recent times for a particular type of unsuccessful group to appear with greater frequency. This group seeks to displace its antagonist and relies on ideological appeals without selective incentives, it lacks bureaucratic organization, and, although not itself a user of constraints as a means of influence, it experiences attack by hostile authorities.

REFERENCES

Ash, Roberta. *Social Movements in America*. Chicago: Markham, 1972.

Galenson, Walter. *The CIO Challenge to the AFL*. Cambridge, Mass.: Harvard University Press, 1960.

Lipsky, Michael. *Protest in City Politics*. Chicago: Rand-McNally, 1970.

McDonald, David J. *Union Man*. New York: Dutton, 1969.

Schattschneider, E. E. *The Semi-Sovereign People*. New York: Holt, Rinehart and Winston, 1960.

chapter nine

The Limits of Pluralism

The study of social protest has only recently emerged from the straightjacket of collective behavior. Under this stultifying tradition, the questions addressed in this book have been largely ignored by American social science. The classical perspective is one in which organized groups seek goals, mobilize resources, and employ strategies, but social movements merely express reactions by the victims of social pathology. Their cries and emotional expressions are viewed as signals of the stresses and strains of society. They react, frequently violently, sensing, without really understanding, the larger social forces which buffet them.

Social movements, in this view, are one product of social disorganization; other products include suicide, criminal behavior, and additional symptoms of a social system in trouble. The participants in social movements are the uprooted. Aminzade (1973, p. 4), a critic of this view, summarizes it for purposes of contrast with an alternative.

> The disrupting effects of large-scale social change, such as migration and urban population growth, involve a breaking apart of social bonds due to the uprooting of persons from traditional communities, which disorients individuals and leads them into disorderly, and sometimes violent, political action. The focus is upon the social disorganization and disintegration produced by the rapid pace of struc-

tural change, which leads to deviant behavior, such as crime, suicide, and political violence. . . . Implied in the model is the mass society notion that the most alienated and disoriented individuals are most likely to join the ranks of the revolution and that collective political violence is essentially an anomic phenomenon.

The collective behavior tradition has produced its prophets such as Eric Hoffer (1951) as well as its serious theorists. Hoffer's treatment has helped to spread many of the basic ideas, albeit in a simplified form, to a large and receptive audience. His central theme is the fundamental irrationality of participation in mass movements. "For men to plunge headlong into an undertaking of vast change, they must be intensely discontented yet not destitute. . . . They must also have an extravagant conception of the prospects and potentialities of the future. Finally, they must be wholly ignorant of the difficulties involved in their vast undertaking. Experience is a handicap" (Hoffer, p. 7).

Mass movements, in Hoffer's argument, offer a substitute for individual hope. They attract the frustrated, those whose present lives are irremediably spoiled. "A man is likely to mind his own business when it is worth minding. When it is not, he takes his mind off his own meaningless affairs by minding other people's business." Participants deal with the frustrations of their present lives by dwelling on what are essentially fantasies about the future. The content of the fantasies is of secondary importance. "The frustrated follow a leader less because of their faith that he is leading them to a promised land than because of their immediate feeling that he is leading them away from their unwanted selves. Surrender to a leader is not a means to an end but a fulfillment. Whither they are led is of secondary importance" (Hoffer, p. 116).

Hoffer is an extreme representative of the collective behavior tradition; he virtually ignores the social conditions that produce the behavior he describes. But other more sophisticated proponents still rely on such psychological states as loss of identity and alienation as the intervening mechanisms in their explanation. Even in the more complex versions, people are unaware of what it is that energizes them to act, and their actions are not directed at the underlying conditions that produce the alienation or anxiety.

Mass behavior, Kornhauser argues (1959) is characterized by a focus of attention on objects that are "remote from personal experience and daily life. . . . Concern for remote objects tends to lack the definiteness, independence, sense of reality, and responsibility to be found in concern for proximate objects." Furthermore, the mode of response to these remote objects is direct and unmediated by social relationships. "People act directly when they do not engage in discussion on the matter at hand, and when they do not act through groups in which they are capable of persuading and being persuaded by their fellows." Mass behavior also "tends to be highly unstable, readily shifting the focus of attention and intensity of response."

The most sophisticated statement of the collective behavior perspective is Smelser's *Theory of Collective Behavior* (1963). Although his complex argument appears very different from the crudities of a Hoffer, it is nevertheless kin. In this version, it is assumed that all political actors will sometimes search for solutions to intractable problems by raising the level of generality. This, in itself, is normal and rational. What distinguishes collective behavior is the phenomenon of "short-circuiting." Intervening steps are jumped as the actor moves from a highly generalized and abstract component of action directly to a source of strain. The short-circuit is made for members of a movement by means of what Smelser calls a "generalized belief." Generalized beliefs are distinguished from other kinds of political beliefs by their failure to specify how we get from the abstract norm or value being questioned to the concrete situations that are producing a problem.

A generalized belief is a myth by which to mobilize people. It contains elements of magical thinking and omnipotence. "The proposed reform will render opponents helpless, and will be effective immediately. . . . Because of this exaggerated potency, adherents often see unlimited bliss in the future if only the reforms are adopted. For if they are adopted, they argue, the basis for threat, frustration, and discomfort will disappear" (Smelser, p. 117). For all his sophistication, then, Smelser retains a sharp distinction between the essentially rational action of routine politics and the oversimplified "generalized beliefs" by which participants in mass movements are moved to act.

The collective behavior paradigm, then, rests on a distinction between the politics of social movements and the politics of conventional groups and organizations — mainstream political parties, lobbies, and interest groups. The actors who engage in these two types of behavior are seen as different species. Conventional groups act to achieve goals rather than reacting to express distress. For such creatures, it is perfectly appropriate to ask about the means of influence they employ to achieve their goals, their coalitions, where they get resources and how they manage them, their skill in negotiation and the like.

Pluralist theory is closely linked to this collective behavior tradition; it is the other side of the coin. Its actors are groups that engage in bargaining to achieve goals. The central process of pluralist politics is exchange. You scratch my back and I'll scratch yours, and, in the end, we'll all get some of what we want. Besides this kind of essentially rational, interest-oriented politics there is the other kind—an irrational, extremist politics, operating on a symbolic level with distant and highly abstract objects. The analysis of this kind of politics is left for the social psychologists whose intellectual tools prepare them to understand the irrational.

Part of the appeal of the collective behavior paradigm is its serviceability as an intellectual weapon to discredit mass movements of which one is critical. It has great versatility. It can, for example, be used by conservative critics of revolutionary movements such as Gustave LeBon (1896).

> By the mere fact that he forms part of an organized crowd, a man descends several rungs in the ladder of civilization. Isolated, he may be a cultivated individual; in a crowd, he is a barbarian—that is, a creature acting by instinct. He possesses the spontaneity, the violence, the ferocity, and also the enthusiasm and heroism of primitive beings, whom he further tends to resemble by the facility with which he allows himself to be impressed by words and images—which would be entirely without action on each of the isolated individuals composing the crowd—and to be induced to commit acts contrary to his most obvious interests and his best known habits. . . . Taken separately, the men of the French Revolutionary Convention were enlightened citizens of peaceful habits. United in a crowd, they did not hesitate to give their adhesion to the most savage proposals, to guillotine individuals most clearly innocent, and, contrary to their interests, to renounce their inviolability and to decimate themselves" (LeBon, pp. 32–33).

It can be used equally well to discredit the frightening fascist movements of the 1920s and 1930s. Who could quarrel with an explanation that depicted the followers of a Hitler or Mussolini as irrational victims of a sick society? Books such as *The Authoritarian Personality* (Adorno, et al., 1950) and *Escape from Freedom* (Fromm, 1941) were hailed as benchmarks of social science achievement.

With the advent of the cold war and the shift of concern to the appeal of communism, many were delighted to find such a handy intellectual apparatus, all cranked and ready to be applied. Authoritarianism was reinterpreted to fit the "extreme" left as well as the "radical right." Former communists were seen to convert to new "authoritarian" belief systems, not under a barrage of intense normative pressure and external sanctions, but from an unconscious psychological insecurity that made them seek certainty. The collective behavior tradition has proved itself highly durable.

Then came the Movement of the 1960s. It is undeniably arrogant, of course, to preempt the capital M for the particular movement that one participates in. But it seems equally undeniable that what Ash (1972) calls the "penumbra" of this set of related challenges blanketed the campuses of America. It created an atmosphere, a set of concerns and issues, that defined the political agenda of those who lived and worked in its ambience.

Many of the intellectual workers operating in this ambience became active participants in the challenges. They marched on picket lines to boycott chain stores that discriminated or went to the South to work on voter registration; they organized teach-ins and marched against the war in Vietnam; they organized rent strikes or sit-ins for open enrollment, elimination of ROTC, or many other specific issues. And if they didn't actively participate, they talked to many who did.

This was not a felicitous circumstance for the continuing acceptance of the collective behavior paradigm. Some, of course, found the politicized atmosphere on campus appalling and destructive and were ready to trot out the old intellectual weapons against this latest threat to political civility (cf. Feuer, 1969). But others, more sympathetic to the Movement, were hardly ready to embrace an explanation that would tar themselves and many friends.

Movement sympathizers and participants such as Flacks (1967), Z. Gamson et al. (1967), and Keniston (1968) were quick to produce evidence on student activists that severely undercut any explanation based on malintegration and personal pathology. Paige (1972), Caplan and Paige (1968), and the social scientists of the Kerner Commission (1968) were equally quick to produce evidence discrediting such explanations of urban rioters. The "riff-raff" theory, characteristic of the McCone Commission report on the Watts riot, was dispatched in short order.

If the collective behavior paradigm seemed so inadequate to deal with the challenges that one experienced at first hand, perhaps it was equally questionable for other movement phenomena normally viewed at a distance with hostility — for example, McCarthyism. I have full sympathy and admiration for those who lived through the trauma and the viciousness of the McCarthy era and were not too cowed to fight back. The threat was real, and I can understand how beleaguered social scientists turned quite naturally to an intellectual apparatus that had apparently made sense of the rise of fascism and used it to discredit Joe McCarthy's followers under the guise of social science explanation. However, work by Rogin (1967), Polsby (1960), and others suggests that this classical approach does not explain the phenomenon very well at all.

This view would have it that McCarthy drew his basic support, not from established, traditionally conservative groups, but from the alienated. McCarthy was seen as a prototypical demagogue appealing to the mass of people for direct support over the heads of their established leaders. He mobilized those individuals who were psychologically vulnerable, splitting apart existing coalitions and upsetting conventional group alignments.

Plausible as it may sound, this view of the McCarthy phenomenon is apparently false. Rogin's work strongly suggests that there was less to McCarthyism than met the eye. Without searching below the surface for hidden frustrations, the bulk of McCarthy's support can be accounted for by taking the issues at face value. On the basis of county voting records, poll data, and other evidence, Rogin concludes that "McCarthy capitalized on popular concern over foreign policy, communism and the Korean War, but the animus of McCarthyism had little to do with any less political or more developed *popular* anxieties. . . . McCarthy did not split apart an elite, the parts of which had been equally conservative before him. He rather capitalized on an existing liberal/conservative split within the existing Republican elite" (1967, pp. 216, and 220). Polsby's (1960) analysis of poll data points in the same general direction. Party affiliation is the single best predictor of support for McCarthy — Democrats opposed him and Republicans supported him. Rogin concludes from his own review, "In these polls, as in the data reported by Polsby, no other single division of the population (by religion, class, eduation, and so forth) even approached the party split" (p. 234). Rogin rejects the notion that McCarthy was sustained primarily by the vague discontents of frustrated groups. "McCarthy had powerful group and elite support. He did not mobilize the masses at the polls or break through existing group cleavages. . . . Communism and the Korean War played crucial roles" (p. 268). The issues on which McCarthy mobilized support were apparently real ones for his followers, not merely symbolic of private anxieties.

The collective behavior apparatus also proved a convenient one for liberals in explaining the support for Senator Barry Goldwater in 1964. It was frequently assumed that the early supporters of Goldwater were anomic, institutionally detached "cranks," neofascists, or "infiltrators" into the Republican Party. "Little old ladies in tennis shoes" became the popular phrase to capture the lunatic fringe imagery.

McEvoy (1971) has demonstrated that the evidence sharply contradicts this image of the Goldwater phenomenon. Pre-convention supporters of Goldwater were compared on a number of variables with those who ultimately voted for him even though they had preferred another nominee prior to the convention. The early Goldwater supporters were significantly higher on such variables as church attendance, income level, and education. They were more likely to be married. Furthermore, they were much higher in past participation in Republican party politics. Finally, they exhibited average-to-low levels of objective status discrepancy. None of this evidence suggests lack of attachment; on the contrary, early Goldwater supporters seem to be strong conservatives with social support and respect from their friends and neighbors.

RESOURCE MANAGEMENT: THE NEW LOOK AT SOCIAL PROTEST

There are now an increasing number of scholars who have begun reexamining social protest without the incubus of the collective behavior paradigm. The assumptions of the new look have begun to emerge more and more explicitly in their work as they attempt to test its explanatory power on a wide range of collective actions. This book draws sustenance from and hopefully contributes to this growing literature.

Oberschall (1973) has made the most comprehensive effort to state that alternative to the collective behavior approach. He begins with the concept of resources.

In ordinary everyday activity, at work, in family life, and in politics, people manage their resources in complex ways: they exchange some resources for other resources; they make up resource deficits by borrowing resources; they recall their earlier investments. Resources are constantly being created, consumed, transferred, assembled and reallocated, exchanged, and even lost. At any given time, some resources are earmarked for group ends and group use, not just individual use. All of these processes can be referred to as "resource management."

Group conflict in its dynamic aspects can be conceptualized from the point of view of resource management. Mobilization refers to the processes by which a discontented group assembles and invests resources for the pursuit of group goals. Social control refers to the same processes, but from the point of view of the incumbents or the group that is being challenged. Groups locked in conflict are in competition for some of the same resources as each seeks to squeeze more resources from initially uncommitted third parties (p. 28).

The discontented are no more nor less rational than other political actors.

The individuals who are faced with resource management decisions make rational choices based on the pursuit of their selfish interests in an enlightened manner. They weigh the rewards and sanctions, costs and benefits, that alternative courses of action represent for them. In conflict situations, as in all other choice situations, their own prior preferences and history, their predispositions, as well as the group structures and influence processes they are caught up in, determine their choices. Indeed, many are bullied and coerced into choices that are contrary to their predispositions. The resource management approach can account for these processes in a routine way (p. 29).

Charles Tilly and his collaborators have been major developers of this approach and have made especially fertile use of it in explaining specific collective actions. The Tilly strategy has been to spawn a number of different studies using historical data on various European countries. The studies are united by a common theoretical framework, set of guiding questions, and great care in the systematic coding and analysis of the basic historical data used to test their propositions.

Groups are viewed as "forming and dissolving, mobilizing and demobilizing, formulating and making claims, acting collectively and ceasing to act, gaining and losing power, in response to changes in five sets of variables: (1) articulated group interests, (2) prevailing standards of justice, (3) resources controlled by groups and their members, (4) resources controlled by other groups (especially governments) and (5) costs of mobilization and collective action" (Tilly, 1973, pp. 6–7; also cf. Tilly "Revolutions and Collective Violence," 1974). Collective actions are "conceptualized as organizational phenomena which occur, not merely because of widespread discontent with war, unemployment, or whatever, but because organizations exist which make possible the channeling and expression of that discontent into concerted social action" (Aminzade, 1973, p. 6).

In place of the old duality of extremist politics and pluralist politics, there is simply politics. The American Medical Association and Students for a Democratic Society are not different species but members of the same species faced with different political environments. All political groups are assumed to have certain collective goals. These goals are not necessarily the same as the goals of the individuals who join them. A person may become active in the Republican Party because he seeks camaraderie and fellowship and is pulled in by friendship networks; because he is motivated by ideological concerns; because he finds in his allegiance to the party a meaningful way of dealing with a confusing world; because he seeks material rewards, status and contacts; or because he seeks an opportunity to exercise power over his fellow men. Most of these reasons would apply as well to joining the Peace and Freedom Party.

The collective goals of political actors rather than the personal goals of members are assumed to be the relevant part of an explanation of political behavior. Whatever the personal motivation of members, the Republican Party has certain goals of its own. These can be recognized by their status as internal justifications in the group. Should the party take action A or B? One answers by reference to certain end-states—for example, gaining political power—which are recognized by other members as justifications, regardless of their personal goals. Collective goals set the criteria for deciding on collective actions.

Similar reasoning applies to social movement actors. They have certain collective goals, and one can make sense of their actions partly by reference to these end-states. They are seen as essentially instrumental in their behavior. This does not mean that they always act in their best interest. They may make mistakes because of poor diagnosis of their political environment, unwise use of resources, and poor organization. They are no different in this respect from the Republican Party, although they may make more or fewer mistakes because of the different political environment and strategic imperatives they face.

Rebellion, in this view, is simply politics by other means. It is not some kind of irrational expression but is as instrumental in its nature as a lobbyist trying to get special favors for his group or a major political party conducting a presidential campaign. As Aminzade puts it, "The resource management model views revolutionary violence as an extension or continuation, in a particular form, of everyday, nonviolent political activity. An event of collective violence is conceptualized, not as a sudden and unpredictable outburst or eruption of heretofore latent tensions or frustrations which take their manifest form in an organizational vacuum, but rather as the outcome of a continuous process of organizational activity" (p. 5).

The absence of rebellion is in need of explanation as much as its presence. Tilly observes that "collective violence is one of the commonest forms of political participation. Why *begin* an inquiry into [the subject] . . . with the presumption that violent politics appear only as a disruption, a deviation, or a last resort? Rather than treating collective violence as an unwholesome deviation from normality, we might do better to ask under what conditions (if any) violence disappears from ordinary political life." He goes on to suggest several reasons why one should hesitate "to assume that collective violence is a sort of witless release of tension divorced from workaday politics: its frequent success as a tactic, its effectiveness in establishing or maintaining a group's political identity, its normative order, its frequent recruitment of ordinary people, and its tendency to evolve in cadence with peaceful political action" (Tilly, 1973b).

Large scale structural changes such as urbanization and industrialization are important not because they create disorganization but because they "strongly affect the number, identity, and organizations of the contenders which in turn determine the predominant forms and loci of conflict. In the short run, the magnitude of conflict depends on an interaction of the tactics of contenders and the coercive practices of the government. In the longer run, the magnitude of conflict depends on the established means by which contenders can enter and leave the polity, and the frequency with which entries and exits actually occur" (Tilly, 1970, p. 4).

The form that protest takes is viewed as the result of an interaction. Confusion on this issue "has led most analysts to jump far too quickly from the fact that a riot occurred to the investigation of why such individuals turned to violence." In fact, the standard sequences for violence occurring are (a) "A group representing a contender for power offers a public show of strength or performs a symbolic act which implicitly lays claim to disputed power and another rival group challenges, which leads to fighting of some sort between the groups and finally to the intervention of repressive force," or (b) "A group representing a contender for power (especially a non-member of the polity) performs an act which lays claim to disputed power, and repressive forces intervene directly to counter that claim" (Tilly, 1970, 26–27). "Whether violence occurs or not [in collective action] depends largely on whether members of one group decide to resist the claims being made by members of another group" (Tilly, 1973a, p. 6).

There are, in this paradigm, some important distinctions to be made among different kinds of political actors. What I have called here "challenging groups" are special kinds of actors with a set of problems that are peculiar to the class. Established groups must maintain the loyalty and commitment of those from whom they draw their resources; challenging groups must create this loyalty. Both attempt influence but established actors have resources routinely available for use and have different relationships to other important political actors.

Powerless groups have special kinds of strategic problems. They cannot call on existing resources but must create their own on the basis of mass support. Or, if the supporting population is not sufficient, they must find ways of bringing allies to their cause. As Lipsky (1968) writes, "The 'problem of the powerless' in protest activity is to activate 'third parties' to enter the implicit or explicit bargaining arena in ways favorable to the protestors. This is one of the few ways in which they can 'create' bargaining resources."

The central difference among political actors is captured by the idea of being inside or outside of the polity. Those who are inside are *members* whose interest is vested—that is, recognized as valid by other members. Those who are outside are challengers. They lack the basic prerogative of members—routine access to decisions that affect them. They may lack this because it is denied them in spite of their best efforts or because their efforts are clumsy and in-effectual. Precisely how entry into the polity operates is a matter for empirical study as in this book.

IMPLICATIONS FOR PLURALIST THEORY

Pluralist theory is a portrait of the inside of the political arena. There one sees a more or less orderly contest, carried out by the classic pluralist rules of bargaining, lobbying, logrolling, coalition formation, negotiation, and compromise. The issue of how one gets into the pressure system is not treated as a central problem. Crenson (1971, p. 179) writes:

> Where there is pluralism, it is argued, there is likely to be competi-tion among political leaders, and where leaders must compete with one another, they will actively seek the support of constituents. A leader who fails to cultivate public support runs the risk of being thrust aside by his rivals when the time comes to submit himself and his policies to the judgement of the electorate. . . . The pluralistic or-ganization of the political elite, therefore, helps to assure that the great bulk of the population will enjoy a substantial amount of indi-rect influence in the making of almost all public decisions, even though it seldom participates directly in the making of any public decision.

Since no fundamental distinction is made between insiders and outsiders, there is little sensitivity to the differences in their politi-cal imperatives. Differences in political situation are treated as dif-ferences in character, between rational actors pursuing interests and irrational actors expressing frustration with social conditions.

The results presented in earlier chapters contradict pluralist im-agery at a number of crucial points. First of all, when we examine the behavior of challengers rather than members, we do not find any connection between success and the means of influence pre-scribed for members. On the contrary, those who are unruly have the most notable success. A willingness to use constraints, includ-ing violence in some cases, is associated with gaining membership and benefits, not with its opposite. This is only true for groups with certain kinds of goals, but it cannot be said that, in general, viola-tion of the rules of pluralist politics is self-defeating for challengers.

The same point can be made with respect to the use of social control strategies by members against challengers. The restraint which pluralist theory claims for political actors does not cross the boundaries of the polity. One uses only limited means against members, but challengers are fair game for a whole gamut of social control techniques. The rules are regarded as just; hence, their violation gives license for repression. Righteous indignation is available to fuel the faint-hearted and to ease the overly scrupulous conscience.

In fact, the set of activities symbolized by Watergate can best be understood in these terms. The Nixon administration introduced an innovation of a special and limited sort: means of political combat that were normally reserved for challengers were applied to members. Nixon was able to claim, with justification, that wire-tapping, burglary, the use of agents provocateur, and the use of the Justice Department and the FBI as a weapon to harass were all practices employed by previous administrations. The special genius of the Nixon administration was to bring these techniques inside the political arena and to direct them at members, thereby causing great indignation among many who had tolerated their use against political pariahs.

The results here also challenge the pluralist assumption that those with a collective interest to pursue will organize to pursue it. The theory of public goods shows that there is nothing natural about the ability to organize successfully. Its achievement is an accomplishment that can and frequently does elude a group that is poor in resources and can offer its members few if any selective incentives.

A member of the polity may need to wheel and deal, but a challenger should be prepared to stand and fight. If the group threatens strong interests of members and is not ready for combat, it is likely to find itself extremely vulnerable to attack and defeat. Members bargain with other members; with persistent challengers, they are prepared to fight and to destroy or ultimately to yield if the fight proves more costly than the stakes warrant.

The pluralist image, then, is a half-truth. It misleads us when applied to the relations between political challengers and members of the polity. The appropriate image for this political interaction is more a fight with few holds barred than it is a contest under well-defined rules. Lowi (1971, p. 53) says it very well. "The history of the United States is not merely one of mutual accommodation among competing groups under a broad umbrella of consensus. The proper image of our society has never been a melting pot. In bad times, it is a boiling pot; in good times, it is a tossed salad. For those who are *in,* this is all very well. But the price has always been paid by those who are *out,* and when they do get in they do not always get in through a process of mutual accommodation under a broad umbrella of consensus."

Some of these unruly and scrappy challengers do eventually become members. One might be tempted to conclude from this that the flaw in the pluralist heaven is, after all, rather exaggerated. Entry is not prohibited for those with the gumption, the persistence, and the skill to pursue it long enough. But this is, at best, cold comfort. Beyond the unsuccessful challengers studied here there may lie others unable to generate enough effort to mount even a visible protest. If it costs so much to succeed, how can we be confident that there are not countless would-be challengers who are deterred by the mere prospect?

REFERENCES

Adorno, Theodore W.; Frenkel-Brunswik, Else; Levinson, Daniel J.; Sanford, R. Nevitt. *The Authoritarian Personality.* New York: Harper & Row, 1950.

Aminzade, Ronald. "Revolution and Collective Political Violence: The Case of the Working Class of Marseille, France, 1830–1871." Working Paper #86, Center for Research on Social Organization. Ann Arbor: University of Michigan, October 1973.

Ash, Roberta. *Social Movements in America.* Chicago: Markham, 1972.

Caplan, Nathan S. and Paige, Jeffery M. "A Study of Ghetto Rioters." *Scientific American,* August 1968, 219:15–21.

Crenson, Matthew A. *The Unpolitics of Air Pollution.* Baltimore: Johns Hopkins Press, 1971.

Feuer, Lewis. *The Conflict of Generations.* New York: Basic Books, 1969.

Flacks, Richard W. "The Liberated Generation: An Exploration of the Roots of Student Protest." *Journal of Social Issues,* July 1967, 23:52–75.

Fromm, Erich. *Escape from Freedom.* New York: Rinehart, 1941.

Gamson, Zelda F.; Goodman, Jeffery; and Gurin, Gerald. "Radicals, Moderates, and Bystanders during a University Protest." Paper presented at American Sociological Association meeting, San Francisco, August 1967.

Hoffer, Eric. *The True Believer.* New York: Harper & Row, 1951.

Keniston, Kenneth. *Young Radicals.* New York: Harcourt, Brace, and World, 1968.

Kerner Commission. *National Advisory Commission on Civil Disorders: Final Report.* New York: Bantam, 1968.

Kornhauser, William. *The Politics of Mass Society.* New York: Free Press, 1959.

LeBon, Gustave. *The Crowd.* London: Ernest Benn, 1896.

Lipsky, Michael. "Protest as a Political Resource." *American Political Science Review,* December 1968, 62:1144–58.

Lowi, Theodore J. *The Politics of Disorder.* New York: Basic Books, 1971.

McEvoy, James III. *Radicals or Conservatives: The Contemporary American Right.* Chicago: Rand-McNally, 1971.

Oberschall, Anthony. *Social Conflict and Social Movements.* Englewood Cliffs, N.J.: Prentice-Hall, 1973.

Paige, Jeffery M. "Political Orientation and Riot Participation." *American Sociological Review,* October 1971, 36:810–20.

Polsby, Nelson W. "Toward an Explanation of McCarthyism." *Political Studies* October 1960, 8:250–71.

Rogin, Michael Paul. *The Intellectuals and McCarthy: The Radical Specter.* Cambridge, Mass.: M.I.T. Press, 1967.

Smelser, Neil J. *Theory of Collective Behavior.* New York: Free Press, 1963.

Tilly, Charles. "From Mobilization to Political Conflict." Center for Research on Social Organization. Ann Arbor: University of Michigan, March 1970.

———— "Collective Action and Conflict in Large-Scale Social Change: Research Plans, 1974–78." Center for Research on Social Organization, Ann Arbor: University of Michigan, October 1973a.

———— "The Chaos of the Living City." Herbert Hirsch and David C. Perry (eds.), *Violence as Politics.* New York: Harper and Row, 1973b.

———— "Revolutions and Collective Violence," in Fred I. Greenstein and Nelson W. Polsby, *Handbook of Political Science,* Vol. 3. Reading, Mass.: Addison-Wesley, 1974.

The 53 Challenging Groups: A Brief Description

The members of the sample of challenging groups are very briefly identified and described below. The dates following the name represent the beginning and end of the period of challenge. The beginning is usually marked by the year in which the group was formed or, in some cases, began a new burst of organizing activity after an inactive period. The end is more complicated and to some degree arbitrary (see pp. 30–31). It is sometimes marked by the disappearance of the group and sometimes by the resolution of active conflict with its target. The outcome of the group's challenge is also listed.

1. American Association of University Professors (1914–22)

A group that attempted to mobilize university professors for the achievement of academic freedom and, more specifically, over the right of trustees to fire teachers and for the establishment of definite rules of tenure. *Co-optation.*

2.   *American Free Trade League (1869–72)*

A group that attempted to mobilize wage-earners along the eastern seaboard and western farmers for the repeal of high tariffs. *Preemption.*

3.   *American Committee for the Outlawry of War (1921–29)*

A group that attempted to mobilize a middle-class reform constituency for American support for a treaty that would make war illegal under international law. The period of challenge ended with the ratification of the Pact of Paris (the Kellogg-Briand Pact) by the United States Senate. *Full response.*

4.   *National Brotherhood of Baseball Players (1885–91)*

A group that attempted to mobilize professional baseball players for the achievement of greater benefits for this group. *Collapse.*

5.   *Brotherhood of the Kingdom (1892–1915)*

A group that was part of the social gospel or social Christianity movement of the late 19th and early 20th century. They attempted to mobilize Christians for a redirection of the energies of the church toward the improvement of social conditions in this world. *Collapse.*

6.   *Social Revolutionary Clubs (Anarcho-Communists) (1880–87)*

A group that based its program on European socialist thought, in particular, the Bakunin wing. It attempted to mobilize primarily German immigrant workers for the abolition of the wage system and the system of private property more generally and to replace them with its particular vision of socialist organization. After initial hesitation, the group chose to support the eight-hour day movement and participated with many others in the meeting in the Haymarket in Chicago on May 4, 1886, in which a bomb was thrown killing a policeman. The leaders of the group were blamed for the incident, tried as accessories to murder, and four were executed. *Collapse.*

7.   *National Urban League (1910–30)*

A group that attempted to mobilize a black and white middle-class reform constituency for efforts to improve the living conditions of urban blacks, particularly migrants from the rural South to the industrial centers of the North. *Full response.*

8. *United Brotherhood of Carpenters and Joiners of America (1881–1912)*

A group that attempted to mobilize carpenters and other wood workers for the achievement of greater benefits for this group. *Full response.*

9. *International Seamen's Union of America (1892–1921)*

A group that attempted to mobilize seamen for the achievement of greater benefits for this group. *Co-optation.*

10. *National Union for Social Justice (1934–36)*

A group, led by the "radio priest" Father Coughlin, that attempted to mobilize working-class Catholics, small farmers, and the masses of unemployed for the achievement of inflationary monetary policies through a variety of means. *Collapse.*

11. *Amalgamated Association of Street and Electrical Railway Workers (1892–1921)*

A group that attempted to mobilize streetcar and trolley workers for the achievement of greater benefits for this group. *Full response.*

12. *American Birth Control League (1921–37)*

A group, led originally by Margaret Sanger, that attempted to mobilize a middle-class reform constituency of women for the greater acceptance of birth control and more specifically to influence legislation affecting this goal. *Collapse.*

13. *American Labor Union (1902–5)*

A group that attempted to mobilize industrial workers for industrial unionism and socialist political goals. The group was an important forerunner of the I.W.W. *Preemption.*

14. *American Federation of Labor (1881–1935)*

A group that attempted to mobilize workers in a variety of trades and industries for the achievement of legislative and political support for the labor movement. *Full response.*

15. *Revolutionary Workers League (Revolt) (1938–43)*

A splinter group of left-wing Trotskyists that attempted to mobilize industrial workers, especially those in the automobile, steel, and maritime industries, for the replacement of the existing economic and political system with a socialist system. *Collapse.*

16. *American Republican Party (Native American Party) (1843–47)*

A nativist group that attempted to mobilize urban native-born Protestants against the rising economic and political power of Catholic immigrants. *Collapse.*

17. *League of Deliverance (1882)*

A nativist group that attempted to mobilize West Coast workers to prevent the employment of Chinese labor. *Full response.*

18. *National Student League (1931–35)*

A group, formed by former members of the Student League for Industrial Democracy, that attempted to mobilize university students for the achievement of an antiwar, antiracist, and antifascist political program. It also concerned itself with campus issues such as the achievement of a free student press and the elimination of compulsory R.O.T.C. *Collapse.*

19. *German-American Bund (1936–43)*

A group that attempted to mobilize the German-American population for the achievement of an American political system along National Socialist lines. *Collapse.*

20. *Brotherhood of the Cooperative Commonwealth (1896–1914)*

A group that attempted to mobilize socialist workers and other sympathizers to gain political control of the state of Washington through establishing cooperative settlements there that would eventually become an electoral majority. *Collapse.*

21. *National Female Anti-Slavery Society (1832–40)*

A group that attempted to mobilize a reform constituency of

middle-class, northern white women to achieve the abolition of slavery. *Collapse.*

22. *American Student Union (1935–41)*

A group, formed by former members of the National Student League and the Student League for Industrial Democracy, that attempted to mobilize university students behind a broad and somewhat changing set of leftist political goals. *Co-optation.*

23. *Young People's Socialist League #1 (YPSL I) (1915–19)*

This group mounted two separate challenges, separated by a period of inactivity, which are treated here as independent challenges (cf. #44). The group was formed by members of the Socialist Party and attempted to mobilize young workers and students toward the achievement of socialist political and economic goals. *Collapse.*

24. *Grand Eight Hour Leagues (1865–72)*

A group that attempted to mobilize primarily skilled workers for the support of eight-hour day legislation. *Preemption.*

25. *Order of Railway Conductors (1885–1934)*

A group that attempted to mobilize railway conductors for the achievement of greater benefits for this group. *Full response.*

26. *American Proportional Representation League (1893–1932)*

A group that attempted to mobilize a middle-class reform constituency for the adoption of proportional representation as a means of breaking the power of urban political machines. *Preemption.*

27. *International Longshoreman's Association (West) (1934–48)*

Two separate challenges are included under the name of the ILA (cf. #49). Although a West Coast branch of the ILA existed before 1934, under Harry Bridges it became essentially an independent union with open defiance of the national president of the union. This challenge deals with the attempt of the group to mobilize West Coast longshoremen for the achievement of greater benefits for this group. *Full response.*

28.   International Association of Machinists (1888–1935)

A group that attempted to mobilize machinists for the achievement of greater benefits for this group. *Full response.*

29.   League of American Wheelmen (1880–1905)

A group that attempted to mobilize bicycle owners and riders to remove restrictions on the use of the bicycle. Later it became a major participant in the good roads movement. *Full response.*

30.   American Federation of Teachers (1916–37)

A group that attempted to mobilize elementary and secondary school teachers for the achievement of greater benefits for this group. *Full response.*

31.   Church Peace Union (1914–45)

A group that attempted to mobilize the religious community in support of American participation in the League of Nations and later the United Nations. *Full response.*

32.   Bull Moose Party (Progressive Party) (1912–16)

A group that attempted to mobilize progressives of both parties for the election of Theodore Roosevelt to the Presidency. *Co-optation.*

33.   Packinghouse Workers Organizing Committee (1937–43)

A group that attempted to mobilize meatpackers for the achievement of greater benefits for this group. *Full response.*

34.   United Hebrew Trades (1888–1910)

A group that attempted to mobilize Jewish immigrant workers in different industries for the achievement of greater benefits for this group. *Full response.*

35.   Tobacco Night Riders (1906–11)

A group that attempted to mobilize tobacco farmers of the black patch area to achieve control of the marketing of tobacco and to break the power of the tobacco trust. *Preemption.*

36.   United Sons of Vulcan (1858–73)

A group that attempted to mobilize boilers, puddlers, and other iron workers for the achievement of greater benefits for this group. *Full response.*

37. Steel Workers Organizing Committee (1936–42)

A group that attempted to mobilize steelworkers for the achievement of greater benefits for this group. *Full response.*

38. March on Washington Committee (1942)

A group that attempted to mobilize urban blacks for the elimination of racial discrimination in employment. The period of this particular challenge was essentially over after President Roosevelt issued an executive order establishing a Fair Employment Practices Committee (FEPC). *Full response.*

39. Prison Discipline Society (1825–30)

A group that attempted to mobilize a middle-class reform constituency for the adoption of the "Auburn-system" of prison organization. *Full response.*

40. Christian Front against Communism (1938–42)

A group, led by Father Coughlin, that attempted to mobilize a broad-based, predominantly working-class Catholic constituency behind a program of isolationism and neutrality in the developing European conflict, anti-Communism, and anti-Semitism. *Collapse.*

41. American Party (1886–88)

A nativist group that attempted to mobilize a constituency of predominantly young workers and white-collar employees to achieve greater restrictions on immigration and naturalization. *Collapse.*

42. Communist Labor Party (1919–20)

A group, formed by delegates from the left-wing caucus of the Socialist Party (the so-called Gitlow-Reed faction), that attempted to mobilize industrial workers for the establishment of a communist state in America. *Collapse.*

43. Dairymen's League (1907–20)

A group that attempted to mobilize dairy farmers for the achievement of benefits for this group. *Co-optation.*

44. *Young Peoples Socialist League, #2 (YPSL II) (1929–54)*

This group began a renewed challenge with the onset of the stock market crash and the depression (cf. #23). It attempted to mobilize young workers and students toward the achievement of socialist political and economic goals. *Collapse.*

45. *Independence League (1905–10)*

A group, formed by William Randolph Hearst, to mobilize a middle-class reform and working-class constituency behind a variety of reform goals to be achieved through Hearst's acquisition of political power. *Collapse.*

46. *Progressive Labor Party (1887)*

A group that attempted to mobilize workers for the election of socialist political candidates. *Collapse.*

47. *Federal Suffrage Association (1892–1920)*

A group that attempted to mobilize middle-class women in support of a constitutional amendment giving women the right to vote. The period of challenge ended with the ratification of the federal suffrage amendment. *Full response.*

48. *Society for the Promotion of Manual Labor in Literary Institutions (1831–33)*

A group that attempted to mobilize a middle-class reform constituency to improve the physical fitness of students in colleges, theological seminaries, and other institutions by introducing programs of physical labor into the curriculum. *Preemption.*

49. *International Longshoreman's Association (East) (1892–1933)*

A group that attempted to mobilize dockworkers for the achievement of benefits to this group. This challenge (cf. #27) focuses on efforts on the East Coast, Great Lakes, and Gulf district. *Full response.*

50. *Union Trade Society of Journeymen Tailors (1833–36)*

A group that attempted to mobilize journeymen tailors for the achievement of benefits to this group. *Collapse.*

51. *International Workingmen's Association (First International) (1869–76)*

This group, the first real Marxist effort in America, attempted to mobilize a constituency of immigrant workers and American intellectuals to achieve the organization of the working class into trade unions and cooperative societies looking ultimately toward the building of a socialist state. *Collapse.*

52. *American Anti-Slavery Society (1833–40)*

A group that attempted to mobilize a middle-class male reform constituency for the abolition of slavery. *Collapse.*

53. *North Carolina Manumission Society (1816–34)*

A group that attempted to mobilize religious white southerners, especially Quakers, to achieve the elimination of slavery through a program of voluntary granting of freedom by slave-holders. *Collapse.*

appendix b

Compiling the Sampling Frame

The sampling frame consisted of a gross list of some 4,500 cards, compiled from the indexes of a series of general and specialized histories. A coder went through each index and listed on a separate card every formal organization — for example, General Motors or the United Automobile Workers — and every collective behavior episode — for example, "Raid on Harper's Ferry" or "Bonus Marchers." High reliabilities were achieved between independent coders using this procedure.

We began with a list of types of social movements or protest groups plus some general bibliographic sources, especially *The Harvard Guide to American History* and *A Guide to the History of the United States*. The categories were agricultural, labor, ethnic (including immigrant), women, religious, prohibition (temperance), nativist, reform, professional, business and commerce, conservation, black, utopian, socialist and communist, peace, veterans, rightist, radicals, cranks and crackpots, sports and recreation, and education. Our concern was that every challenging group be covered by at least one of these categories, and it mattered not at all if it fit into several. Through this method, we developed a bibliography of some 75 books.

We started the list or file with some general sources: six volumes and a supplement of the *Dictionary of American History, The Oxford Companion to American History,* Richard Morris' *An Encyclopedia of American History* and Louis Filler's *A Dictionary of Social Reform.* From here, we proceeded to the more specialized histories within each category.

A list of the entries from each new source was checked against the growing file to avoid making duplicate entries. If some group was already in the file, the additional source was recorded on its card. As each source was used, a tally was made of the percentage of new entries it provided to the file. The final dozen sources, from several different categories, yielded an average of 10 percent new entries, and all were below 20 percent. In examining these new entries, we gained the strong impression that very few, if any, would actually meet the criteria for a challenging group. To check this impression, we did further investigation on the final 20 new entries. Seven were local chapters of larger groups that had already been included. One was not a formal organization or collective behavior episode. Two were federally funded institutions or projects. One was a pseudonym for the Ku Klux Klan, which, of course, was already included, and five were local organizations dealing strictly with local issues. The remaining four were international organizations or organizations in other countries whose activities were not directed primarily at American antagonists. Thus, none of the last 20 new entries actually added any challenging groups to the gross list.

The entries in the gross list consisted of valid entries—that is, challenging groups—and blanks, where a blank was defined as any card entry which, upon investigation, did not meet the criteria for a valid entry.

Our sampling procedure consisted of drawing a random sample, actually an interval sample, of 11 percent of the cards, 467 in all. Once we filtered the challenging groups from these cards and dealt with problems of duplication and multiple listings, our valid entries represented a random sample of all valid entries in the gross file. Of course, having filtered only those cards that were selected in our sample, we could not produce a total list of valid entries, but it was quite unnecessary to do so.

The process of culling valid entries from blanks was quite time-consuming. Many could be eliminated quickly by simple inspection —for example, "socialism," "industrial-unionism," "Paris Commune," "class struggle doctrine," "U.S. Department of Agriculture." Others required further investigation. Frequently, it was sufficient to turn to the source that yielded the index listing, but some cases required many hours of library work before we learned that they failed to meet one of the criteria described in the text (see pp. 16–18).

It was important to give each challenging group only one card. Many groups were known by a variety of names, and, to insure that such a group had only one chance of entering the sample, it was necessary to adopt conventions that would link it with a unique name. If there was a most common or popular name for the group, we used this. If there were two or more equally common names, we treated the longest name as the unique name. A sample card was considered a valid entry only if it contained the unique name of the challenging group. The file was also checked for exact duplicates, something which could occur through error. If another card appeared for the same group, the chosen card was given a .5 probability of remaining in the sample to correct for the double probability that it had inadvertently been given earlier.

In the case of cards with collective behavior episodes, we attempted to associate these with some sponsoring organization whenever this was appropriate—for example, the Butte Miner's Strike was associated with the Western Miner's Union. The card with the name of the organization was designated as the unique way for the challenging group to enter in such cases. In theory, a collective behavior listing might have yielded a challenging group, in the absence of any appropriate organization listing, but this, in fact, never occurred. Thus, all of our final sample listings are organizations.

Although the file was considered complete when we drew the sample, it was perfectly possible to add new entries that we might uncover in the course of the research. All we required is that every additional entry be given the same .11 probability of entering the sample as earlier entries. For example, we drew the card, "Good Roads Movement." On investigating this entry, we discovered seven different organizations that had some involvement, not necessarily all challenging groups. Some were in the file already, and some were not. Those that were not in the file were given cards and a .11 probability of coming in, and one of these, the League of American Wheelmen, was selected and qualified as a challenging group.

Sometimes a challenging group goes into a period of dormancy and then mounts a new mobilization effort after a quiet period of five years or more. These are new challenging groups with independent careers, and we do not wish to eliminate them merely because they use the same banner as an earlier challenge. The Ku Klux Klan is a good example. The revived Klan in the 1920s took the name of the earlier organization, but it might have chosen another. The choice of a name by a group should not be a criterion for its inclusion or exclusion. To handle this, we included all challenges under the same name as independent challenging groups, treating a new burst of activity after a dormant period of five years or longer as an additional sample entry. The KKK did not fall into the sample, but two cases of this type did. The International Longshoreman's Association was involved in two rather separate challenges, one begun in the 1890s, concentrating mainly in the East and the Great Lakes region, and another in the 1930s under Harry Bridges' leadership on the West Coast. The Young People's Socialist League also had two separate efforts, one during the period of World War I and one during the depression. Each of these single entries, then, yielded two separate challenging groups, since only in this manner would the separate efforts have an equal probability of inclusion.

When the culling and duplicate eliminating process was completed, we were left with 64 apparently valid entries. We were able to get sufficient information on 83 percent of them, but 11 eluded our efforts. We know a little about these nonrespondents, and they apparently are valid entries, although it is quite possible that if we knew more some of them could be discarded. Of course, if we knew more, we could presumably have completed protocols on some of them and added them to our analysis. The 11 are briefly described below:

1. *The Order of Secularists*

A secret society of the 1860s intent on creating a proper climate for social reform in the United States by propagating atheism. It was composed primarily of German immigrants and included among its members Fredrich Sorge, the dominant figure in the First International and the so-called Father of Marxism in America. It was successfully secret, and there is inadequate information on its nature and activities.

2.   *Lower Taxes, Less Legislation League*

A reform group of the progressive era.

3.   *Union of Russian Workers*

A major target of the Palmer Raids following World War I. Many of its members were among the 249 aliens deported in January 1920.

4.   *Lithuanian Socialist Federation*

A group of Lithuanian immigrants, perhaps no more than a branch or satellite of the Socialist Party without independent status, but we do not know.

5.   *Corn Belt Committee*

A group of midwestern farmers who wanted Congress to institute a plan to pay farmers their cost of production plus profit, regardless of market prices.

6.   *The American Negro Labor Congress*

A group that attempted to organize blacks into unions during the 1920s.

7.   *National Christian Citizenship League*

One of several Christian Socialist organizations during the 1880s and 1890s.

8.   *National Direct Legislation League*

A group formed in the 1890s to gain various governmental reforms.

9.   *Seamen and Harbor Workers Union*

An alleged communist-front organization of the 1930s.

10.   *Philadelphia Journeymen House Painters Association*

A group of the 1860s that was involved in efforts to form a city-wide trades assembly. It may have been localized, but journeymen house painters were not; therefore, it can not be ruled invalid out of hand.

11. National Labor Defense Council

A group of civil libertarians formed in 1917 to support the International Workers of the World (IWW) and other labor groups that were harassed by the government.

It is conceivable that enough information could be found on some of these groups but not within the resources available to this project. They do not appear to be concentrated in any particular time period although none are pre-Civil War. Nor are they of any particular type. They are well distributed over occupational, reform, and socialist categories although right-wing groups are apparently not represented among these nonrespondents.

We conclude this appendix with the list of sources used to compile the gross sampling list or card file.

Agriculture

Benedict, M. R., *Farm Policies of the United States, 1790–1950*
Shannon, Fred A., *American Farmer's Movements*
Taylor, Carl C., *The Farmer's Movements, 1620–1920*
Hicks, J. D., and Saloutos, T., *Agricultural Discontent in the Middle West*
Buck, S. J., *Agrarian Crusade*
Taylor, Carl C., *Rural Life in the United States*
Gates, Paul E., *The Farmers Age*

Labor

Saposs, *Left-Wing Unionism*
Commons, J. R., et al., *History of Labor in the United States*, vols. 2, 3, 4
Fine, Nathan, *Labor and Farmer Parties in the United States — 1828–1928*
Dulles, R. F., *Labor in America*
Yellen, Samuel, *American Labor Struggles*

Ethnic Groups (Immigrants)

Higham, John, *Strangers in the Land*
Brown, F. J., and Roucek, J. S., *One America*
Commons, J. R., *Races and Immigrants in America*
Hansen, M. L., *The Immigrant in American History*
Kohler, M. J., *Immigration and Aliens in the United States*
Wittke, Carl, *We Who Built America*

Women

Stanton, Elizabeth, et al., *History of Woman Suffrage,* 6 vols. Many other listings are included in books on social reform with sections on women's movements.

Religious Groups

Stokes, Anson P., *Church and State in the United States*
Sweet, W. W., *Religion in America*

Prohibition Groups (Temperance)

Colvin, D. L., *Prohibition in the United States*
Asbury, Herbert, *The Great Illusion*

Nativist

Higham, John, *Strangers in the Land*
Billington, R. A., *The American Protestant Crusade 1800–1860*

Reform Groups

Filler, Louis, *A Dictionary of Social Reform*
Aaron, Daniel, *Men of Good Hope — A Story of American Progressives*
Nye, R. B., *Midwestern Progressive Politics*
Warbasse, J. P., *Co-operative Democracy through Voluntary Association*
Filler, Louis, *Crusaders for American Liberalism*
"The Arbitrator," William Floyd, ed., *Social Progress*
Daniels, John, *Co-operation — An American Way*

Professions

Warren, Charles, *A History of the American Bar*
Packhard, F. R., *History of Medicine in the U.S.,* Vol. II

Business and Commerce

Shultz, W. J. and Caine, *Financial Development of the United States*
Studenski, Paul and Kross, *Financial History of the U.S.*

Conservation

Van Hise, C. R., *Conservation of Our Natural Resources*

Black (and Other Racial, Religious, and Ethnic Minorities)

Frazier, E. F., *The Negro in the United States*

McWilliams, Carey, *A Mask for Privilege—Anti-Semitism in America*

Rose, Arnold and Caroline, *America Divided*

Franklin, J. H., *From Slavery to Freedom*

Bennett, Lerone, Jr., *Before the Mayflower: A History of the Negro in America*

Utopias

Bestor, A. E., *Backwoods Utopias*

Tyler, A. F., *Freedom's Ferment—Phases of American Socialism to 1860*

Socialism and Communism

Hillquit, Morris, *History of Socialism in the United States*

Gitlow, J. B., *The Whole of Their Lives*

Egbert, et al., *Socialism and American Life*

Kipnis, Ira, *The American Socialist Movement 1897–1912*

Cannon, J. P., *History of American Trotskyism*

Herreshoff, David, *American Disciples of Marx*

Quint, H., *The Forging of American Socialism*

Bimba, Anthony, *History of the American Working Class*

Peace

Curti, M. E., *Peace or War—The American Struggle 1636–1936*

War, Veterans, and Rightist Groups

Evan, Wallace, *Patriotism on Parade*

Harrison, Gordon, *Road to the Right*

Rossiter, Clinton, *Conservatism in America*

Wector, Dixon, *When Johnny Comes Marching Home*

Radicals, Cranks and Crackpots

Preston, William, *Aliens and Dissenters*

Chafee, Z., Jr., *Free Speech in the United States*

Adamic, Louis, *Dynamite—the Story of Class Violence in America*

Greer, Thomas H., *American Social Reform Movements, Their Pattern Since 1865*

Destler, Chester M., *American Radicalism*

Jaker, F. C., *Doubters and Dissenters — Cataclysmic Thought in America 1885–1918*

David, Henry, *The History of the Haymarket Affair*

Allen, Frederick Lewis, *Only Yesterday*

Sports

Dulles, R. F., *America Learns to Play*

Education

Knight, Edgar W., *Education in the United States*

Butts, R. F. and Cremin, *A History of Education in American Culture*

The Questionnaire

1. Background Information

1.1   Name of compiler.

1.2   Sample listing from card file (e.g., "anarcho-communists").

1.3   Constituency of the CG.[1]

1.4   Check list of criteria for inclusion as a CG. Compiler must note whether the sample entry passes all validity tests, including checks for duplication.

1.5   Aliases. Other names by which the CG was known.

1.6   Time reference points. Significant events in the CG's history which can be used to establish time boundaries for its activities and relationships (e.g., strike begins at X company: June 12, 1937 = T3).

1.7   Sources used in compiling the protocol. Note any general biases or overall point of view.

1.8   Background briefing. A short (one page) general description to orient the coder.

1.9   Context of the times. A brief description of the historical context in which the CG arose.

1.10   Primary antagonists of the CG.

---

[1] We will employ the abbreviation CG for challenging group.

2. Law Enforcement System

This section of the questionnaire deals with the relationship between the CG and the *law enforcement system*. This latter term is intended to include police, special investigatory agencies (e.g., FBI, Narcotics Agents, etc.), and the judicial system. The police may be the local police department or sheriff's office, state police, or federal law enforcement officials. The investigatory agencies referred to above are those connected with law enforcement and do not include legislative investigating committees or regulatory commissions which are covered elsewhere. The judicial system includes everything from local magistrates through the Supreme Court.

The questionnaire sometimes makes use of the term police as a shorthand for this entire system. If relevant information is discovered about parts of the law enforcement system other than the police, this should be included also—for example, the military, national guard, and militia.

2.1   Salience of law enforcement system.[2]

How much emotional salience, positive or negative, did the *local* law enforcement system have for the CG? How much emotional salience did the *supralocal* system have? To what extent was either an object of intense feeling or of little or no concern?

2.2   Legal police activity short of arrest.

How much legal police activity short of arrest was directed toward the CG? To what extent were CG members investigated, subjected to surveillance, and interrogated?

2.3   Arrests.

To what extent were CG members subject to arrest?

2.4   Illegitimate police activity.

How much illegal police activity or activity beyond the spirit of the law was directed at the CG?

2.5   Police protection of CG.

How adequate was police protection of CG members and rendering of normal police services? How adequately did police respond to requests for aid? How adequately were CG members protected from hostile third parties?

---

[2] Under each question the compiler was given a set of additional instructions concerning the information sought. These additional instructions are not included here but are available on request.

2.6   Collusion against.

How much collusion was there between the law enforcement system and hostile third parties? To what extend did police and judges hold membership in hostile third-party groups? To what extent was there informal collusion or sympathy with hostile third parties?

2.7   Collusion with.

How much joint membership was there between police or judges and CG? To what extent was there informal collusion or sympathy with CG?

2.8   CG trust in police.

What was the CG attitude toward the police?

2.9   CG trust in courts.

What was the CG attitude toward the courts?

2.10   Hostile CG activity against police.

How much hostile activity did the CG direct against members of the law enforcement system? To what extent did they verbally or physically attack the police and attempt to harass them?

2.11   Use of courts as resource.

How much use did the CG make of the judicial system as a resource in bringing about social change?

3. Public Agencies

This section deals with the relationship between the CG and public agencies other than law enforcement agencies. Examples of such agencies are HEW, HUD, the Department of Agriculture, the State Education Commission, and the Interstate Commerce Commission. The President, any governor, and other office holders in the executive branch are included here.

3.1   Salience of public agencies.

Were public agencies relevant to the aims or tactics of the CG? If so, in what ways?

3.2   Influence attempts on public agencies by CG and allies.

What influence attempts on public agencies were made by CG or, on behalf of CG, by some ally?

3.3   Influence attempts on public agencies by hostile third parties.

Was influence applied to public agencies by hostile third parties aimed at regulating the behavior of the CG?

3.4   Favorable actions by public agencies.

What actions by public agencies occurred which were favorable to the CG?

3.5   Unfavorable actions by public agencies.

What actions by public agencies occurred which were unfavorable to the CG?

4.   (This section was integrated into section 3 above).

5.   Communication System

This section deals primarily with the relationship of the CG to the mass media. However, where relevant, it also includes information on communication in face-to-face interaction.

The mass media include (at different periods) TV, radio, newspapers, newsmagazines, newsreels, and books, among others. We *exclude* here publications of the CG — that is, internal house organs — aimed at their constituency although press releases and statements designed to reach a general audience would be included.

In face-to-face communication, we also focus on messages intended to reach an audience *outside* of the constituency. Examples here would include communication through sermons in churches, through political meetings, through talks at private clubs, employee gatherings, and other organizational functions. Typically, this includes a leader of the CG talking to some audience outside of the constituency in which he or she is justifying the demands or explaining the grievances of the CG. (An example would be that of black militants lecturing to predominantly white audiences.)

5.1   Salience of the CG for the mass media.

To what extent were the mass media aware of the CG and its activities? How much attention did they give it? How much attention did they give to the problems raised by the CG?

5.2   Salience of communications system for CG.

To what extent did the CG show sensitivity or concern about the communications system? To what extent did it see communications with an outside audience as relevant and important?

5.3   Public relations attempts by CG.

To what extent did the CG carry out activities aimed at influencing the content and extent of publicity about them?

5.4   Public relations attempts directed against CG by antagonists.

To what extent did antagonists carry out activities aimed at influencing the content and extent of publicity about the CG and its activities?

5.5   Favorableness of mass media coverage.

How favorable or unfavorable was the content of the media coverage?

5.6   Favorableness of public opinion toward CG.

To what extent was the CG a focus of conversation and concern for large segments or all of the general public? What was the dominant attitude(s) toward the CG, its leaders, goals, activities, etc.? Was there consensus or polarization among those concerned in their attitudes toward the CG?

6.   Electoral System

This section deals with the CG experience with the electoral process. This experience can be mediated through one of the established major parties, through an existing third party, or through the creation of a new third party. We also include here experiences which are a precondition to participation in electoral politics — namely CG activities aimed at enfranchisement (or antagonist activities aimed at disenfranchisement.)

6.1   Salience of electoral politics.

To what degree were electoral politics seen as a relevant arena of political action by CG?

6.2   Primary relationship to political party system.

What type of political party experience did the CG regard as most relevant for its participation in electoral politics — working through a major established political party, through an existing third party, through an emerging third party, or through preparty activity?

6.3   Influence attempts by CG on major political parties.

In what ways did the CG attempt to gain influence through the medium of a major political party?

6.4   Influence attempts by CG with respect to third parties.

In what ways did the CG attempt to gain influence through the medium of a third party?

6.5   Influence attempts by CG aimed at enfranchisement.

To what extent did the CG attempt to remove barriers to constituency participation in the electoral process and to encourage such participation?

6.6   Influence attempts by antagonists aimed at limiting degree of success of CG participation in electoral politics.

To what extent did antagonists attempt to influence CG participation in electoral politics or to limit its success?

6.7   Degree of inclusion of CG and constituency in major political parties.

To what extent was the CG successful in electing candidates to offices on major party tickets? To what extent were they successful in winning party offices and positions? To what extent did major parties adopt the CG program as part of its platform? To what extent did a major party become an agent of CG interests?

6.8   Degree of third party success.

To what extent did CG-backed third parties win electoral success? To what extent did major party platforms attempt to preempt issues and solutions promoted by CG-backed third parties?

7.   Legislative Bodies

This section deals with the relationship between the CG and legislative bodies at any level of the governmental system. Legislators sometimes function in other roles—for example, as political party leaders or as partisans for interest groups on one or another issue. We focus on them here in their role as lawmaker. The level may range from city council through Congress.

7.1   Salience of legislative bodies to CG.

To what degree was legislative action seen as relevant for CG aims and tactics? To what extent were actions initiated by legislative bodies relevant?

7.2   Influence attempts on legislative bodies by CG and allies.

To what extent and in what way did the CG attempt to influence legislation?

7.3   Influence attempts on legislative bodies by hostile third parties.

To what extent and in what way did hostile parties attempt to promote legislation against CG interests?

7.4   Favorable actions by legislative bodies.

To what extent did favorable legislative actions occur affecting either the CG or its constituency?

7.5   Unfavorable actions by legislative bodies.

To what extent did unfavorable legislative actions occur affecting either the CG or its constituency?

8.   Private Interest Groups and Other Challenging Groups

This section covers interest groups in two separate roles — as the targets of CG influence (i.e., as antagonists) and as allies or enemies in influencing some other target (i.e., as partisans). We also distinguish between private groups with well-established support from some constituency and those that are themselves challenging groups in a state of attempted mobilization. In summary, we consider three different relationships of the CG in this section of the questionnaire:

A.   Private established interest groups as antagonists or targets of influence.

B.   Established private interest groups as allies or enemies in the CG's efforts.

C.   Other challenging groups as allies or enemies in the CG's efforts.

A.   *Private Interest Groups as Antagonists*

8.1   Salience of specific private groups as antagonists.

To what extent was some private group the major target of CG activity — for example, as a private company or an industry is for many labor groups?

8.2   Influence attempts on private targets by CG and its allies.

To what extent and in what way did the CG attempt to influence a private target?

8.3   Influence attempts on private targets by hostile third parties.

To what extent and in what way did hostile third parties attempt to influence the private target to act against CG interests or wishes?

8.4   Favorable actions by a private group as antagonist.

To what extent did the private target take action affecting favorably either the CG or its constituency?

8.5   Unfavorable actions by a private group as antagonist.

To what extent did the private target take action affecting unfavorably either the CG or its constituency?

B.   *Established Interest Groups as Allies or Enemies*

8.6   Alliance ideology.

What beliefs did the CG hold about the importance and desirability of alliances with other groups?

8.7   Scope enlargement attempts short of formal alliance.

To what extent did the CG attempt to draw other interest groups into the conflict as honest broker or sympathizer?

8.8   Alliance attempts by CG toward established interest groups.

To what extent did the CG approach established interest groups in efforts to gain their support for the changes sought by the CG?

8.9   Alliance attempts by established interest groups toward CG.

To what extent was the CG offered support by established interest groups?

8.10   Actual alliance formed between CG and established interest groups.

What working relationships were developed and maintained between the CG and established interest groups?

8.11   Hostile activity directed by CG against established interest groups.

To what extent did the CG attempt to injure, discredit, or undermine established interest groups that it regarded as enemies?

8.12   Attempts by CG to appeal "over the head" of established interest groups to win support of their constituency.

To what extent did the CG attempt to woo away the membership of established interest groups against the desires of the leaders of such groups?

8.13   Hostile activity directed by established interest groups against CG.

To what extent did established interest groups attempt to injure, discredit, or undermine the CG?

8.14   Coordination of hostile activity by established interest groups.

To what extent were the hostile activities described in 8.13 (if any) coordinated and organized among different hostile third parties.

C.   *Other CGs as Allies or Enemies*

8.15   Alliance attempts by CG toward other CGs.

To what extent did the CG attempt to work with other CGs in a more general social movement?

8.16   Alliance attempts by other CGs toward focal CG.

To what extent did other CGs attempt to include the focal CG in its activities?

8.17   Actual alliances formed between CG and other CGs.

To what extent did the CG actively participate with other CGs as part of a larger social movement?

8.18   Hostile activity directed *by* CG at other CGs.

To what extent did the CG attempt to undermine or retard the mobilization efforts of other CGs?

8.19   Hostile activity directed *at* CG by other CGs.

To what extent did other CGs attempt to undermine or retard the mobilization efforts of the focal CG?

9.   Attributes of CG

The focus on the questionnaire shifts at this point from the relationship between the CG and other groups to its internal characteristics — its leadership, organizational structure, tactics, and ideology, among others.

9.0   Growth.

What was the peak membership of the CG and its size at different points in time?

9.1   Formal goals.

What was the generalized belief or end-state on the basis of which the CG attempted to mobilize its constituency?

9.2   Beliefs about tactics and strategy.

What are the means by which the CG hoped to achieve its goals?

9.3   Actual means of influence used.

What was the predominant means of influence employed by the CG?

9.4   Beliefs about resources needed and their availability.

What did the CG view as its primary resources, and how did it hope to obtain these in sufficient amount?

9.5   Actual availability of resources.

What resources were available to the CG and in what quantities?

9.6   Leadership structure and change.

To what extent was the CG led by a single dominant leader with a strong personal following or by a more collective leadership without a single dominant figure?

9.7   Quality and skill of leadership.

To what extent were leaders experienced and skilled in performing different leadership functions?

9.8   Bureaucratization.

To what extent were rules of membership and operation of the CG formalized in a constitution or similar document?

9.9   Secrecy.

To what extent were activities of the CG carried on secretly?

9.10   Diffusion of internal authority.

How large a group within the CG was involved in internal decision-making?

9.11   Factional strife.

How frequent and severe were internal divisions in the CG?

10.   Attributes of Constituency

While the previous section focused on the active or organizational component, the challenging group, this section focuses on the underlying constituency of the CG.

10.1   Type of solidarity.

What social characteristics distinguished the constituency of the CG?

10.2   Geograpical concentration.

To what extent was the constituency geographically dispersed or concentrated?

10.3   Socio-economic status.

To what extent was the constituency predominantly middle class or lower class in background?

10.4   Rural-urban location.

To what extent was the constituency predominantly rural or urban?

10.5   Physical distinctiveness.

To what extent did the constituency have physical characteristics or mannerisms, such as foreign accents, that set them apart from the surrounding population?

10.6   Degree of nonmovement interaction.

To what extent did the constituency members interact with each other outside of the context of CG activities?

10.7   Subcultural distinctiveness.

To what extent did the constituency form a distinctive subculture with a common life style, norms, and values?

11. Boundary Relations between CG and Its Constituency

11.1 Degree of commitment required by members.

To what extent did CG participation call for total involvement by members rather than partial and spare-time involvement?

11.2 Social distance between CG leaders and average member of constituency.

To what extent did CG leaders come from essentially the same social background and life experiences as the average member of their constituency?

11.3 Ease of constituency members becoming involved in CG activites.

How permeable were the boundaries of the CG for a would-be activist?

11.4 Degree of competition faced by CG.

To what extent did the CG have a monopoly on efforts to mobilize its constituency, and to what extent did it face competition from CGs with similar aims?

12. Outcome Variables

Outcome is viewed from two angles, the degree of acceptance that the CG gains as an organization and the degree of new advantages that the beneficiary obtains. The new advantages that are diffused to the beneficiary are examined twice, once at the time point at the end of the challenging period of the CG and again over the fifteen-year time span that follows the end of the period of challenge. The end of the period of challenge is called TN, and TN + 15 years is called TU. For a discussion of how TN is determined, see Chapter Three (pp. 30–31).

A. Acceptance of CG

12.0 Organizational fate of the challenge.

What was the state of the CG as an organization at TN?

12.01 Inclusion of CG leaders and members in the organization of its antagonist.

To what extent were CG leader(s) and/or members offered positions of power, prestige, and/or influence within the formal structure of the antagonist?

12.1 Formal recognition.

To what extent was the CG extended formal recognition by its antagonist as a spokesman for the CG's beneficiary?

12.2   Acceptance through negotiation.

To what extent was acceptance of the CG implied by the willingness of its antagonist to engage in negotiations with it over matters affecting its beneficiary?

12.3   Acceptance through consultation.

To what extent did the antagonist contact the CG to consult with it on matters affecting the beneficiary?

12.4   Antiacceptance and discrediting efforts.

To what extent did the antagonist attempt to deny that the CG was an agent for or representative of the beneficiary?

B.   New Advantages to Beneficiary by TN

12.5   Formal concessions or agreements.

To what extent was the CG able to win specific advantages for its beneficiary through formal agreement or contract?

12.6   Policy changes dealing with stated CG goals – undisputed.

To what extent did policy changes occur which were acknowledged by both the CG and its target to meet explicit grievances?

12.7   Policy changes aiding beneficiary but unconnected with explicit CG grievances – undisputed.

To what extent did policy changes occur which were acknowledged by both the CG and its target to aid the beneficiary.

12.8   Disputed policy changes.

To what extent were there claims that new benefits had been extended which were disputed by one or another protagonist?

12.9   Policy changes decreasing benefits.

To what extent were new policies introduced that decreased benefits to the beneficiary during the period of challenge?

C.   New Advantages to Beneficiary: TN to TU

12.10   Formal concessions or agreements.

To what extent was the CG or its successors able to win specific advantages for its beneficiary through formal agreement or contract from TN to TU?

12.11   Policy changes dealing with stated CG goals – undisputed.

To what extent did policy changes occur which were acknowledged by both the CG, or its successors, and the target to meet explicit grievances during TN to TU?

12.12 Policy changes aiding the beneficiary but unconnected
with explicit CG grievances – undisputed.

To what extent did policy changes occur which were acknowledged by both the CG, or its successor, and its target to aid the
beneficiary from TN to TU?

12.13 Disputed policy changes.

To what extent were there claims that new benefits had been extended which were disputed by one or another protagonist during
TN to TU?

12.14 Policy changes decreasing benefits.

To what extent were new policies introduced that decreased
benefits to the beneficiary during the period between TN and TU?

Basic Codes and Data

Some readers may wish to analyze the data described in this book to address additional issues not discussed here or to check other interpretations of the results. To facilitate this, the basic codes are presented here along with the data on these codes for the 53 groups in the sample. Missing code columns cover identifying information or variables of questionable reliability that have been omitted.

Col. 14: Type of group.

    1. Occupational groups including unions, farmers.   20 (38%)

    2. Reform groups including peace groups, civil rights groups, social gospel groups, abolitionists.   17 (32%)

    3. Socialist groups including leftist student groups.   10 (19%)

    4. Right wing groups including nativist groups.   6 (11%)

Col. 18: Minimal acceptance relationship.

    1. Yes.   21 (40%)

    2. Consultation only.   4 (8%)

    3. No.   28 (53%)

Col. 20: Overall new advantages.

    1. No new advantages.   20 (38%)

    2. Equivocal advantages.   3 (6%)

3.	New advantages.	26	(49%)
4.	Partial and peripheral advantages.	4	(7%)

Col. 21: Combined outcome measure: Unequivocal advantages and minimal acceptance relationship.

		Col. 18	Col. 20		
1.	Full response.	1, 2	3	20	(38%)
2.	Preemption.	3	3	6	(11%)
3.	Co-optation.	1, 2	1, 2, 4	5	(9%)
4.	Collapse.	3	1, 2, 4	22	(42%)

Col. 24: Is violence present in the interaction between the CG and others?

1.	No.	36	(68%)
2.	Yes, undisputed and unequivocal.	15	(28%)
3.	Yes, but disputed or equivocal—for example, only an isolated incident in which a small scuffle broke out with no arrests or serious injuries.	2	(4%)

Col. 25: Did the group use violence either in self-defense or in pursuit of its goals?

1.	No.	44	(83%)
2.	Yes, undisputed and unequivocal.	8	(15%)
3.	Yes, but disputed and equivocal.	1	(2%)

Col. 26: Was the group subjected to violence by others including the police? (Do not include arrests per se unless accompanied by beating or other physical abuse.)

1.	No.	40	(75%)
2.	Yes, by hostile third parties.	4	(8%)
4.	Yes, by police or militia.	7	(13%)
6.	Yes, by both hostile third parties and by police or militia.	2	(4%)

Col. 27: Were group members subject to arrests or other nonviolent constraints by the police?

1.	No.	32	(60%)
2.	Yes, undisputed and unequivocal.	18	(34%)
3.	Yes, but disputed and equivocal.	2	(4%)
4.	Yes, but only in test cases deliberately initiated by the group.	1	(2%)

Col. 28:   Group ideology on violence.
  1.   Rejection, implicit or explicit. Either violence was not an issue and no mention is made of it (it is irrelevant for the CG), or it is mentioned and explicitly rejected, *and* the group does not arm itself, give its members paramilitary training, or in any other way make preparations to defend itself or carry out actions using arms.   46   (87%)
  2.   Acceptance. Either violence is explicitly claimed to be legitimate or necessary under *some* circumstances and/or the group arms itself, gives paramilitary training to its members or in other ways prepares to defend itself or carry out actions using arms.   7   (13%)
Col. 30:   Violence status summary.
  1.   No violence or arrest in history (1 in Col. 24–27).   30   (57%)
  2.   Violence user (2 in Col. 25).   8   (15%)
  3.   Violence recipient (1 in Col. 25 and 2, 4, or 6 in Col. 26).   7   (13%)
  4.   Arrest only (1 in Cols. 25 and 26 and 2 in Col. 27).   8   (15%)
Col. 32:   Target displacement. Was the CG trying to either destroy or replace the target(s) as a way of realizing its goals/demands?
1. or 2.   Yes.   16   (30%)
  5.   No.   37   (70%)
Col. 34:   Public good/private good.
  1.   CG constituents get it especially, not pooled.   27   (51%)
  2.   CG constituents get it especially, but pooled. (Do not code here if #1 is possible.)   16   (30%)
  3.   Everyone gets it and it's pooled. (Do not code if #1 or #2 is possible.)   6   (11%)
  4.   Those who are not part of CG constituency get it especially.   4   (8%)
Col. 35:   More than benefits.
  1.   More than simply boundaries or benefits is at issue.   35   (66%)

    2.   Only boundaries or benefits.   18   (34%)

Col. 37:   Systemic versus local.

    1.   Target of change is system qua system, not merely one element, not one industry or specific institution (e.g., fighting communism or capitalism, achieving world peace or national socialism).   11   (21%)

    2.   Local: a particular and specific institution, organization, or industry (e.g., university administrations, slavery, prisons, etc.).   42   (79%)

Col. 39:   Dominant leader.

    1.   There was a single dominant leader with whom the group was identified. The group could be considered in some sense a vehicle for a single leader.   20   (38%)

    3.   Several prominent leaders; or a single leader but one who is clearly subordinate to group or organization; or a succession of leaders. Group is in no sense a vehicle for a single dominant leader.   33   (62%)

Col. 40:   Secrecy.

    1.   Group practiced secrecy in the form of secret rituals, covert activity, etc. Secrecy is institutionalized and represents more than merely a private planning meeting on occasion.   9   (17%)

    2.   Group did not practice institutionalized secrecy. Include here groups whose only secrecy was maintaining private membership lists. The fact that a group does not publicize every fact about itself is not sufficient for inclusion here.   44   (83%)

Col. 41:   Factionalism.

    1.   No major factional splits in history of the group nor was group born out of a factional split. Internal disputes in group did not result in members leaving, through expulsion or resignation, to set up a new group.   30   (57%)

    2.   Group was born out of factional dispute, but it did not experience any splits during its challenge.   7   (13%)

3. Group was born out of factional dispute and experienced factional splits after birth.   1   (2%)

4. Group not born out of factionalism but experienced it after birth.   15   (28%)

Col. 42: Timing of factionalism — relationship to external attack.

1. No factionalism (1 on Col. 41).   30   (57%)

2. Factionalism prior to attack. Internally generated but external attack follows within two years of factional split or factional birth.   3   (6%)

3. Factionalism but no attack within two years after split or factional birth. Internally generated.   17   (32%)

4. Factionalism after external attack. Factional split or factional birth follows within two years of external attack.   3   (6%)

(Note: external attack is defined as the application of violence, arrest, or other constraints applied to group members by outsiders.)

Col. 44: Written constitution or charter.

1. Written document existed stating both purposes of organization and provisions for operation.   33   (62%)

2. Written document existed stating purposes only but without provisions for operation (e.g., a manifesto).   13   (25%)

3. No written document is known to have existed.   7   (13%)

Col. 45: Formal membership list.

1. Organization maintained a list of members.   38   (72%)

2. No formal list was maintained.   15   (28%)

Col. 46: Full-time employees.

1. CG had more than one full-time paid employee.   29   (55%)

2. CG had one full-time paid employee.   4   (8%)

3. CG had no paid, full-time employees, only volunteers or part-time help.   20   (37%)

Col. 48: Levels of hierarchy.

1. Three or more levels — officers; division,

committee, or chapter heads; rank and file.   31   (58%)

2. Two levels – officers and council; rank and file.   3   (6%)
3. Two levels – officers or leaders and rank and file.   19   (36%)

Col. 50: Size of group at peak.
1. Under 1,000.   11   (21%)
2. 1,000–9,999.   16   (30%)
3. 10,000–99,999.   12   (23%)
4. 100,000 plus.   14   (26%)

Col. 51: Bureaucracy summary code.
1. Full formal bureaucracy (1 on Cols. 44, 45, *and* 48).   24   (45%)
2. Not full formal bureaucracy (not #1 above).   29   (55%)

Col. 56: Electoral system salience. (Code in terms of practice, not simply belief.)
1. Electoral challenge. CG formed third party and/or attempted to elect its members to office and/or to use referenda as a means of reform.   8   (15%)
2. Electoral challenge through existing parties only. Group supported candidates it deemed sympathetic and worked for them or against unsympathetic candidates. (Code here only if #1 is not an appropriate code.)   13   (25%)
3. Nonelectoral challenge. CG took no interest in the electoral system.   32   (60%)

Col. 58: Means of influence.
1. Group accepted in principle *and* made use of constraints as a means of influence in one of the following forms:
   a. Doing injury to persons or property,
   b. Strikes or boycotts,   20   (38%)
   c. Efforts to discredit and humiliate individual enemies by personal vituperation; discrediting efforts are individualized and not simply directed against "the system" or other more abstract targets; ad hominem attacks.

2. Group made use of but never tried to justify constraints in principle, even as a necessary evil.   1   (2%)
3. Group justified, advocated, or accepted as necessary the use of constraints under appropriate circumstances but never got around to actually using them.   10   (19%)
4. Group rejected constraints implicitly or explicitly in both action and belief.   22   (41%)

Col. 59:   Alliances excluding physical attacks and arrest.

Some definitions: *Help* = more than verbal support; some pooling of resources to help the CG. *Hindrance* = more than verbal condemnation; more tangible harassment that hinders the group in its efforts to mobilize and influence. Exclude physical violence and arrests here since they are coded elsewhere. Include, for example, censorship. (Note: Focus here is on help or hindrance in influence. Do not include actions which could be regarded as an outcome measure—for example, legislation which the group is seeking as part of its goals or which deals unfavorably with the issues and causes that the group is pursuing. Include only if it is action which helps or hinders the group in its capacity for influence or mobilization. For example, legislation prohibiting or permitting "yellow dog" contracts would be included; legislation guaranteeing a minimum wage would not.) *Outsider* = not a target of influence and not another CG. Outsider refers to an established interest group or political party or government agency that is not itself the target of change but can, by its actions, help or hinder the efforts of the group.

1. Group received only help from outsiders.   13   (25%)
2. Group received both help and hindrance from outsiders.   5   (9%)

3. Group received neither help nor hindrance from outsiders.   29   (55%)

4. Group received only hindrance from outsiders.   6   (11%)

Col. 60: Help and hindrance summary. (The same as Col. 59 only arrests and violence are added to hindrance.)

1. Help only (1 in Col. 59, 1 in Col. 26 *and* 1 or 4 in Col. 27).   11   (21%)

2. Help and hindrance (2 in Col. 59; *or* 1 in Col. 59 *and* 2, 4, 6 in Col. 26 or 2, 3 in Col. 27).   7   (13%)

3. Neither help nor hindrance (3 in Col. 59 and 1 in Col. 26 and 1 or 4 in Col. 27).   18   (34%)

4. Hindrance only (4 in Col. 59 *or* 3 in Col. 59 *and* 2, 4, 6 in Col. 26 *or* 2, 3 in Col. 27).   17   (32%)
(Note: Col. 26 = subjected to violence; Col. 27 = subjected to arrest.)

Col. 62: Class origins of constituency.

1. Middle class and professional, including wives of same.   13   (24%)

2. Blue-collar workers, manual workers, craftsmen.   21   (40%)

3. Farmers.   3   (6%)

4. Mixture of working class and middle class or workers and farmers.   10   (19%)

5. Students.   2   (4%)

6. Ethnic groups, including blacks.   4   (8%)

Col. 63: Initial resources – sponsorship.

1. No patron.   39   (74%)

2. Yes. Group had wealthy backers who were willing to finance it.   3   (6%)

3. Yes. Group had the patronage of figures of considerable prestige among outsiders, high status patrons. (Refers to more than upper-middle-class status: to people who have reputations as individuals outside of challenge.)   4   (8%)

4. Yes. Group had the patronage of those who occupied important decision-making positions in institutional hierarchies.   5   (9%)

5. Yes. More than one of the above.   2   (4%)
    (Note: Don't include as a patron anyone
    whose status grew out of the challenge it-
    self. Refer only to status prior to the chal-
    lenge.)

Col. 65: Competition — other CGs in the field.
    1. Yes. Other groups existed at the same time
        attempting to appeal to roughly the same
        constituency about similar issues, but not
        necessarily using the same tactics or pro-
        gram.   30   (57%)
    2. No. No real competition from another
        group existed. Include here even if many
        members of the constituency belonged to
        other groups as long as these other groups
        were not offering an *alternative* vehicle. 23   (43%)

Col. 66: Class composition of constituency: sum-
          mary code.
    1. Middle class and students (1 or 5 in Col.
        62).   15   (28%)
    2. Blue collar and ethnic (2 or 6 in Col. 62). 25   (47%)
    3. Farmers (3 in Col. 62).   3   (6%)
    4. Mixed (4 in Col. 62).   10   (19%)

Col. 67: Sponsorship: summary code.
    1. No sponsor (1 in Col. 63).   39   (74%)
    2. Yes. Sponsorship (2–5 in Col. 63).   14   (26%)

Col. 69: Number of antagonists and concerns.
    1. Single type of antagonist and single area of
        concern.   10   (19%)
    2. More than one type of antagonist but a
        single area of concern.   34   (64%)
    3. Single type of antagonist but more than
        one area of concern.   0   (0%)
    4. More than one type of antagonist, more
        than one area of concern.   9   (17%)
        (Note: The "government" as an antagonist
        is considered to be more than one type —
        i.e., code #2 or #4 above.)
            The "emancipation of the working
        class," the "establishment of a socialist
        state," are considered single areas of con-

cern unless specific subgoals are formulated by the group (e.g., elimination of ROTC on campus; staying out of war; establishing an FEPC; etc.).

Col. 70: Selective incentives.
1. Yes. Group provides some form of tangible selective incentive, nonsymbolic, to members before TN. (Code #2 if provided only after TN.)   9   (17%)
2. No. No evidence of any selective incentives beyond such things as emotional satisfaction and social interaction valued for itself.   44   (83%)

Col. 71: Inclusiveness versus exclusiveness.
1. Inclusive organization. Any eligible member who wants to can join. No period of probation or formal induction.   48   (91%)
2. Exclusive. Members are required to go through probationary period or investigation after which they are formally inducted into the group.   5   (9%)

Col. 72: Diffusion versus centralization of internal authority.
1. Centralized. A single center of internal power. This may be a single leader or a group, with or without official authority. Where there are branches or chapters, their freedom of action is clearly limited.   28   (53%)
2. Decentralized. More than one center of power in the organization. May be diffused through membership at large or in chapters and divisions with a considerable amount of freedom of action. Coalition-like.   19   (36%)
3. Probably decentralized. No positive evidence of centralization exists; no dominant leader or other indication of centralization.   6   (11%)

Col. 73: Date of beginning of challenge.
1. Before 1860.   8   (15%)
2. 1860–1879.   3   (6%)
3. 1880–1899.   18   (34%)
4. 1890–1913.   6   (11%)

5.	1914–1928.	7	(13%)
6.	1929–1945.	11	(21%)

Col. 74: Relationship of CG to competitor CGs.

1. CG is less moderate than principal competitor. Advocates or uses more militant means, i.e., constraints, or goals implying higher degree of conflict with antagonist. — 10 (19%)
2. CG is more moderate than principal competitor. — 7 (13%)
3. No difference between CG and competitor or inconsistent differences. Put jurisdictional disputes here. Put here if CG's only claim is that it is more effective than rival without any connotation of greater or lesser militancy. — 13 (25%)
4. No competitor (2 on Col. 65). — 23 (43%)

Column

Group	14	18	20	21	24	25	26	27	28	30	32	34	35	37	39	40	41	42	44	45	46	48	50	51	56	58	59	60	62	63	65	66	67	69	70	71	72	73	74
1. American Association of University Professors	1	2	2	3	1	1	1	1	1	1	5	1	1	2	3	2	2	1	1	1	1	1	2	1	3	4	3	3	1	3	2	1	2	2	2	3	3	5	4
2. American Free Trade League	2	3	3	2	1	1	1	1	1	1	5	2	1	2	3	2	2	1	3	2	1	3	2	2	1	4	1	4	4	3	2	4	2	2	2	3	3	2	4
3. American Committee for the Outlawry of War	2	2	3	1	1	1	1	1	1	1	5	3	2	2	1	2	2	1	3	2	3	3	1	2	2	4	1	1	2	5	1	1	2	2	1	1	5	5	3
4. National Brotherhood of Baseball Players	1	3	1	4	1	1	1	1	1	1	5	1	2	2	1	1	1	1	2	1	3	3	1	2	3	3	3	2	1	1	2	2	1	2	2	1	3	4	4
5. Brotherhood of the Kingdom	2	3	2	4	1	1	1	1	1	1	5	3	2	1	3	2	1	1	2	2	3	3	2	2	3	4	3	3	2	1	2	1	1	1	2	1	2	3	4
6. Anarcho-Communists	3	3	1	4	2	4	1	2	2	3	1	1	1	1	3	2	1	1	2	2	3	3	1	2	3	3	3	4	1	1	2	2	2	2	2	2	2	3	1
7. National Urban League	2	1	3	1	1	1	1	1	1	1	5	2	2	2	3	2	1	1	2	2	3	1	3	1	3	4	1	1	6	4	2	2	2	1	1	1	4	4	4
8. United Brotherhood of Carpenters and Joiners	1	1	3	1	1	1	1	2	1	4	5	1	2	2	1	2	1	1	1	1	1	1	4	1	3	1	3	4	2	1	1	2	1	1	1	1	3	3	3
9. International Seamen's Union of America	1	1	4	3	1	1	1	1	1	1	5	2	2	2	1	2	4	3	2	2	3	3	3	1	3	1	4	2	2	1	1	1	1	1	1	2	2	3	2
10. National Union for Social Justice	4	3	4	4	1	1	1	1	1	1	2	2	1	2	1	2	1	1	2	1	1	1	4	2	1	4	3	3	4	1	2	4	4	4	2	1	1	6	4
11. Amalgamated Assn. of Street & Elec'l Railway Workers	1	1	3	1	2	2	1	2	1	2	5	1	1	2	1	1	1	1	1	1	1	4	4	1	2	1	3	4	2	1	1	1	1	1	1	1	3	3	3
12. American Birth Control League	2	3	1	4	1	1	1	1	1	4	5	1	2	2	1	2	1	1	2	2	3	2	3	2	3	4	4	4	1	1	1	1	2	2	2	1	5	3	3
13. American Labor Union	1	3	3	2	1	1	1	1	1	1	5	1	2	1	3	2	1	3	1	1	1	1	3	2	2	1	3	2	2	1	1	2	2	2	2	1	4	3	1
14. American Federation of Labor	1	1	3	1	1	1	1	1	1	1	5	1	1	2	1	2	4	3	1	1	1	1	4	1	2	1	3	2	2	1	2	2	2	2	2	1	3	3	2
15. Revolutionary Workers League (Revolt)	3	3	1	4	3	1	1	3	2	4	2	2	1	1	3	2	2	2	2	2	3	3	1	2	3	3	2	2	2	1	2	2	2	2	2	3	3	6	3
16. Native American Party	4	3	4	4	2	4	1	3	1	2	2	2	2	2	3	2	2	3	2	2	3	1	3	2	1	2	2	2	4	1	2	4	4	4	1	2	2	1	4
17. League of Deliverance	4	1	3	1	1	1	1	1	2	4	2	2	1	3	1	2	2	1	1	1	2	3	1	2	3	1	3	4	4	1	2	4	1	2	1	1	3	3	4

Group	14	18	20	21	24	25	26	27	28	30	32	34	35	37	39	40	41	42	44	45	46	48	50	51	56	58	59	60	62	63	65	66	67	69	70	71	72	73	74
18. National Student League	3	3	1	4	2	1	4	2	1	3	1	1	1	2	3	2	2	3	1	1	3	1	2	1	3	1	4	4	5	1	1	1	1	4	2	1	2	6	1
19. German-American Bund	4	3	1	4	3	1	1	2	2	4	2	3	1	1	1	1	1	1	2	1	1	1	3	2	2	3	4	4	6	4	1	2	2	2	2	2	1	6	1
20. Brotherhood of the Cooperative Commonwealth	3	3	1	4	1	1	1	1	1	1	2	2	1	2	3	2	4	3	2	1	2	3	2	2	3	4	3	3	2	1	1	2	1	2	2	1	3	3	3
21. National Female Anti-Slavery Society	2	3	1	4	2	1	2	1	1	3	5	4	1	2	3	2	4	4	1	1	3	1	2	1	3	4	4	4	1		2	1	2	2	2	2	2	1	4
22. American Student Union	3	1	1	3	1	1	1	1	1	1	5	1	1	2	3	2	3	3	1	1	1	3	3	1	3	3	3	4	5		2	4	4	4	2	1	2	6	4
23. YPSL I	3	3	1	4	1	1	1	2	1	4	2	2	1	1	3	1	4	4	1	1	3	3	2	2	2	3	3	4	4		1	4	2	2	2	2	2	5	2
24. Grand Eight Hour Leagues	1	3	3	2	1	1	1	1	1	1	5	1	2	2	1	2	1	1	3	2	3	3	1	1	2	4	3	3	4	1	4	4	1	2	2	2	1	2	3
25. Order of Railway Conductors	1	1	3	1	1	1	1	1	1	1	5	1	1	2	3	2	1	1	1	1	1	1	1	3	3	1	3	3	2	1	2	2	1	2	1	2	2	3	2
26. American Proportional Representation League	2	3	3	2	1	1	1	1	1	1	5	2	1	2	3	2	1	1	1	1	1	1	1	1	1	4	1	1	1		2	1	2	2	2	2	1	3	4
27. International Longshoreman's Assn. (West)	1	1	3	1	2	2	6	2	1	2	5	1	1	2	1	2	1	1	3	1	1	1	3	2	3	1	2	2	2	1	2	2	2	2	2	2	1	6	4
28. International Assn. of Machinists	1	3	3	1	1	1	1	1	1	1	5	1	1	2	3	1	1	1	1	1	1	1	4	1	2	1	1	2	2	1	2	2	2	2	2	1	2	3	3
29. League of American Wheelmen	2	2	3	1	1	1	1	4	1	1	5	2	2	2	3	2	4	3	1	1	1	1	4	1	2	4	3	3	4	4	2	1	1	1	1	1	2	3	4
30. American Federation of Teachers	1	1	3	1	1	1	1	1	1	1	5	1	1	2	3	2	4	3	1	1	1	3	3	3	3	4	2	2	1		2	2	2	2	2	2	2	5	1
31. Church Peace Union	2	1	3	1	2	1	1	1	1	1	5	3	2	1	3	2	1	1	1	2	2	2	2	2	3	4	3	3	1	2	2	2	2	2	2	1	1	5	4
32. Bull Moose Party	2	1	1	3	1	1	1	2	1	1	2	2	1	2	1	2	2	3	2	1	1	1	4	2	1	4	1	1	4	3	4	4	2	4	4	1	1	4	3
33. Packinghouse Workers Organizing Committee	1	1	3	1	2	2	2	2	1	2	5	1	2	2	3	2	4	3	1	1	1	3	3	1	3	1	2	2	2		1	2	2	2	2	1	1	6	1
34. United Hebrew Trades	1	1	3	1	2	2	4	2	1	2	5	1	1	2	3	2	1	1	1	1	1	1	4	1	3	1	3	4	6	1	1	1	1	2	2	2	1	3	2
35. Tobacco Night Riders	1	3	3	2	2	2	2	2	2	2	5	1	2	2	1	1	1	1	2	2	3	1	2	2	3	3	3	4	3	1	2	3	1	1	2	2	1	4	4

Group	14	18	20	21	24	25	26	27	28	30	32	34	35	37	39	40	41	42	44	45	46	48	50	51	56	58	59	60	62	63	65	66	67	69	70	71	72	73	74
36. United Sons of Vulcan	1	1	3	1	1	1	1	1	1	1	5	2	2	2	3	1	1	1	1	1	1	1	2	1	3	1	3	3	2	1	2	2	1	2	1	1	2	1	4
37. Steel Workers Organizing Committee	1	1	3	1	2	2	4	2	2	2	5	1	2	2	3	2	1	1	1	1	1	1	4	1	2	1	2	2	2	4	1	2	2	2	2	1	2	6	1
38. March on Washington Committee	2	1	3	1	1	1	1	1	1	1	5	2	2	1	1	2	1	1	1	2	3	3	2	2	3	1	1	1	6	4	2	2	2	1	2	1	6	6	4
39. Prison Discipline Society	2	3	3	1	1	1	1	1	1	1	5	4	2	2	1		1	1	3	1	2	3	2	2	3	4	3	3	1	1	1	1	1	1	1	1	1	1	3
40. Christian Front against Communism	4	3	1	4	2	2	1	2	1	2	2	3	2	2	1	2	2	3	2	2	3	3	4	2	2	1	4	4	2	1	2	2	2	2	2	1	6	3	4
41. American Party	4	3	1	4	1	1	1	1	1	1	2	2	2	2	3		4	3	2	2	3	3	2	2	2	4	3	3	4	3	2	4	2	4	2	2	2	3	4
42. Communist Labor Party	3	3	1	4	1	1	2	2	2	4	2	2	1	2	1	1	2	2	2	2	1	3	3	2	3	3	2	2	2	1	1	2	1	1	2	2	5	4	1
43. Dairymen's League	1	1	4	3	2		2	1	1	3	5	1	2	2	3	2	1	1	1	1	1	1	4	1	3	1	3	4	3	1	2	3	1	2	1	2	4	4	4
44. YPSL II	3	3	1	4	1	1	1	2	1	4	2	1	2	1	3	2	4	3	1	1	3	3	2	2	2	3	3	4	4	1	1	4	1	4	2	1	6	6	3
45. Independence League	2	3	1	4	1	2	1	1	1	1	2	1	1	2	1	2	1	1	2	2	3	3	4	2	1	1	1	1	4	5	1	4	2	4	2	1	1	4	3
46. Progressive Labor Party	3	3	1	1	1	1	1	1	1	1	2	2	2	2	3	2	2	3	2	2	3	3	2	2	1	4	3	3	2	1	1	2	1	4	2	3	3	3	1
47. Federal Suffrage Association	2	2	3	1	1	1	1	2	2	1	5	1	1	1	3	2	2	1	1	1	3	3	1	2	2	4	4	1	1	1	1	1	1	1	2	1	2	3	3
48. Soc. for the Promotion of Manual Labor in Literary Inst.	2	3	3	2	1	1	2	2	2	1	5	3	2	2	3	2	2	1	3	2	2	2	2	2	3	4	1	1	1	2	2	1	2	2	2	1	1	1	4
49. International Longshoreman's Assn. (East)	1	1	3	1	1		1	1	1	3	5	1	2	2	1	2	4	3	3	1	1	4	4	2	3	3	3	3	2	2	1	2	1	1	1	1	3	1	2
50. Union Trade Society of Journeymen Tailors	1	3	1	4	3	4	4	2	1	3	5	4	2	2	3	2	2	3	3	1	3	3	1	2	3	1	3	4	2	1	2	2	2	2	2	3	3	1	4
51. First International	3	3	1	4	1	1	1	1	1	1	5	1	2	1	1	2	4	2	1	2	1	2	2	1	3	3	3	4	2	1	1	2	1	2	2	1	1	2	2
52. American Anti-Slavery Society	2	3	1	4	1	2	1	2	1	3	5	4	1	2	3	2	4	4	1	1	1	1	4	4	3	4	4	4	1	2	1	2	2	2	2	1	2	2	1
53. North Carolina Manumission Soc.	2	3	2	4	1	1	1	1	1	1	5	4	2	2	3	2	4	3	1	1	3	1	2	1	3	4	3	3	3	1	2	3	1	2	2	2	1	1	4

appendix e

Some Negative Results

I have tried in the body of this book to give coherence to a set of results. Readers, of course, may make their own interpretations, and, in some cases, their interpretations may rest on variables that were not discussed. There are basically two reasons why theoretically interesting variables are omitted. By far the most important reason was our frequent inability to extract what we considered meaningful and reliable measures of them. We have tried not to force our data beyond its natural limits.

There was a second reason for exclusion. A few variables that we were able to measure reasonably well yielded equivocal or uninteresting results. Of course, interest and equivocality are not intrinsic characteristics of results but a function of the interpretation one makes. Some readers, making different interpretations, may see more meaning in these results than we have, and they are presented here to allow this possibility.

NATURE OF ANTAGONIST

Some groups such as labor unions directed their challenge primarily in the private sector; others had a set of governmental authorities as a target. This distinction is less than clear-cut. It is quite common for groups to have both public and private antagonists. Some student groups in the 1960s, for example, made the government in Washington the target of action on one occasion, university administration the target on another, and a private corporation such as Dow Chemical the target on a third. Such a mixture is not untypical among our 53 challengers.

Nevertheless, we were able to classify challengers by whether their most frequent or predominant antagonists were in the public or private sector. A little more than half (55 percent) of the groups had predominantly governmental targets. At first glance, challengers with public targets seem to enjoy less success than the others. Only 34 percent won acceptance and 41 percent new advantages, against 62 percent and 58 percent respectively for groups with private targets.

However, these differences can be largely accounted for by the presence of all but two of the 16 groups with target displacement goals among the challengers with public targets (see pp. 41–44). When these groups are removed from the analysis, the results disappear or even reverse themselves. Of the nondisplacing groups with public targets, 60 percent win acceptance, compared to 64 percent of the nondisplacing groups with private targets. The figures for new advantages are 80 percent and 59 percent respectively.

ELECTORAL VERSUS NONELECTORAL CHALLENGERS

Some 21 of the challenging groups attempted to utilize the electoral system at some point during their period of challenge. In some cases this involved forming or supporting a third party, in others supporting or working through existing major parties. The remaining 32 challengers took no particular interest in the electoral system.

There is remarkably little difference in the outcomes between these two groups of challengers: 52 percent of the electoral challengers gained new advantages compared to 47 percent of the others. The advantage lay the other way with respect to acceptance: 38 percent of the electoral challengers gained acceptance compared to 53 percent of the remainder. Note, however, that this difference is partly an artifact of how acceptance was defined. A purely electoral challenger, one whose only target of influence was a set of political offices, was considered accepted only if it enjoyed some electoral success. Thus, there is a degree of noncomparability in the measure of acceptance for some of the electoral challengers that can easily account for the slight difference found.

COMPETITION WITH OTHER CHALLENGING GROUPS

Only 23 groups had the field to themselves; no other challenger was attempting to mobilize a significant part of their constituency at the same time they offered their mobilization efforts. The other 30 groups did not enjoy such a monopoly; for them, other challenging groups existed at the same time attempting to appeal to roughly the same constituency on similar issues. Of course, these rival challengers did not necessarily use the same tactics or program in their appeals.

Again there is a striking lack of difference in success on what seems like a potentially important variable. Exactly half of the groups with competition and 48 percent of the others were successful in gaining new advantages. For acceptance, the figure were 50 percent and 44 percent respectively.

SECRECY

We suspected that secrecy might be positively related to success since it might enhance the ability of a group to wage political combat. Only nine of the challengers practiced secrecy in the form of secret rituals, covert activity, or the like. To be classified as a practicer of secrecy, the practices had to be institutionalized and to represent more than merely a private planning meeting on occasion.

It turns out that secrecy has no apparent relationship to outcome for this sample. Four of the nine secret groups gained new advantages and acceptance; the percentage for the remaining 44 groups is virtually identical.

SOCIAL CLASS ORIGINS

One of the most interesting variables on which to compare groups is the social class origin of their constituency. Is the system more open for challenging groups with a middle-class as opposed to a working-class constituency?

Unfortunately, we found it difficult to get a fully reliable measure of the class composition of many challengers; a good many attempted to appeal across class lines, and our information on their

success in doing so is spotty and incomplete. We were able to identify with reasonable reliability 15 groups that directed their appeal
primarily to middle-class people and/or to college students.

There is almost no difference in the success rate of these groups
when compared to the remainder. Fifty-three percent gained acceptance and a like percentage gained new advantages; for the
others, 45 percent and 47 percent gained acceptance and new advantages, respectively. Even these negligible differences wash out
or are reversed when one controls for target-displacement goals.
Only one of the middle-class-based groups, a student group, attempted to displace its antagonist. Thus, the nonmiddle-class
groups achieve their virtually equal success rate in spite of a siz-
able number of target displacers in their ranks.

When these groups are removed from the analysis, the nonmiddle-class groups actually do better than their middle-class
counterparts. Seventy-four percent gain new advantages compared
to 57 percent of the middle-class challengers. Their greater militancy and combativeness can account for much of the advantage
(see pp. 72–88).

Finally, it is worth noting that middle-class status does not ex-
empt a group from attack. More than a quarter (27 percent) of the
middle-class groups were either the passive recipients of violence
or were subject to arrests, only slightly lower than the 29 percent of
the nonmiddle class groups receiving similar treatment.

bibliography

Adamic, Louis.
    1944   *A Nation of Nations.* New York: Harper & Bros.
Adams, Alice Dana.
    1964   *The Neglected Period of Anti-Slavery in America, 1808–1831.* Gloucester, Mass.: P. Smith.
Adorno, Theodore W.; Frenkel-Brunswik, Else; Levinson, Daniel J.; Sanford, R. Nevitt.
    1950   *The Authoritarian Personality.* New York: Harper & Row.
Agger, Robert; Goldrich, Daniel; and Swanson, Bert E.
    1964   *The Rulers and the Ruled.* New York: Wiley.
Albrecht, Arthur Emil.
    1923   *International Seamen's Union of America: A Study of Its History and Problems.* Washington, D.C.: U.S. Printing Office.
Allen, Lee.
    1950   *100 Years of Baseball.* New York: Bartholomew House.
    1961   *The National League Story: The Official History.* New York: Hill & Wang.
American Federation of Teachers, Commission on Educational Reconstruction.
    1955   *Organizing the Teaching Profession: The Story of the American Federation of Teachers.* Glencoe, Ill.: Free Press.
Aminzade, Ronald.
    1973   "Revolution and Collective Political Violence: The Case of

the Working Class of Marseille, France 1830–1871." Working Paper #86, Center for Research on Social Organization. Ann Arbor: University of Michigan, October.

Anderson, L. F.
  1913 "The Manual Labor School Movement." *Educational Review 46.*

Anson, Adrian.
  1900 *A Baseball Player's Career.* Chicago: Era Publishing.

Ash, Roberta.
  1972 *Social Movements in America.* Chicago: Markham.

Bancroft, Hubert Howe.
  1890 *The Works of Hubert Howe Bancroft, Vol. 24, History of California 1860–90.* San Francisco: History Co.

Barnes, Gilbert H.
  1957 *The Anti-Slavery Impulse, 1830–1844.* Gloucester, Mass.: P. Smith.

Barnes, Gilbert H., and Dumond, Dwight L.
  1934 *Letters of Theodore Dwight Weld, Angela Grimké Weld, and Sarah Grimké, 1822–1844.* New York: D. Appleton-Century.

Barnes, Harry Elmer.
  1918 *A History of the Penal, Reformatory and Correctional Institutions of the State of New Jersey, Analytical and Documentary.* Trenton, N.J.: MacCrellish & Quigley.
  1926 *The Repression of Crime: Studies in Historical Penology.* New York: George H. Doran.

Bartlett, Roland Willey.
  1931 *Cooperation in Marketing Dairy Products.* Springfield, Ill.: C. C. Thomas.

Bassett, John Spencer.
  1898 *Anti-Slavery Leaders of North Carolina.* Baltimore: Johns Hopkins Press.
  1899 *Slavery in the State of North Carolina.* Johns Hopkins University Studies in Historical and Political Science, ser. XVII, no. 7–8. Baltimore: Johns Hopkins Press.

Bean, Walton.
  1968 *California: An Interpretive History.* New York: McGraw-Hill.

de Beaumont, Gustave, and de Tocqueville, Alexis.
  1833 *On the Penitentiary System in the United States, and Its Application in France.* Tr. by Francis Lieber. Philadelphia: Carey, Lea & Blanchard.

Bennett, David H.
  1969 *Demagogues in the Depression: American Radicals and the*

Union Party, 1932–1936. New Brunswick: Rutgers University Press.

Bernheimer, Charles S., ed.
1905   *The Russian Jew in the United States.* Philadelphia: J. C. Winston.

Bernstein, Irving.
1970   *Turbulent Years: A History of the American Worker, 1933–1941.* Boston: Houghton Mifflin.

Billington, Ray Allen.
1963   *The Protestant Crusade, 1800–1860: A Study of the Origins of American Nativism.* Gloucester, Mass.: P. Smith.

Bloom, Bernard H.
n.d.   "Yiddish Speaking Socialists in America: 1892–1905." *American Jewish History,* Vol. 3. n.d.

Bodein, Vernon Parker.
1944   *The Social Gospel of Walter Rauschenbusch and Its Relation to Religious Education.* New Haven: Yale University Press.

Bose, Atindranath.
1967   *A History of Anarchism.* Calcutta: World Press.

Boulware, Marcus H.
1969   *The Oratory of Negro Leaders, 1900–1968.* Westport, Conn.: Negro Universities Press.

Brissenden, Paul F.
1957   *The I.W.W.: A Study of American Syndicalism.* New York: Columbia University Press.

Broderick, Francis L., and Meier, August, eds.
1966   *Negro Protest Thought in the Twentieth Century.* Indianapolis: Bobbs-Merrill.

Brody, David.
1964   *The Butcher Workmen: A Study of Unionization.* Cambridge, Mass.: Harvard University Press.

Brown, Olympia, ed.
1917   *Democratic Ideals: A Memorial Sketch of Clara B. Colby.* n.p., Federal Suffrage Assn.

Butts, R. Freeman, and Cremin, Lawrence A.
1953   *A History of Education in American Culture.* New York: Holt.

Caplan, Nathan S., and Paige, Jeffery M.
1968   "A Study of Ghetto Rioters." *Scientific American,* August, 219:15–21.

Carlson, John R.
1943   *Under Cover.* Philadelphia: Blakiston.

Carlson, Oliver, and Bates, Ernest S.
    1936   *Hearst, Lord of San Simeon.* New York: Viking Press.
Chapman, Maria W.
    1839   *Right and Wrong in Massachusetts.* Boston: Dow and Jackson's Anti-Slavery Press.
Christie, Robert A.
    1956   *Empire in Wood: A History of the Carpenters' Union.* Ithaca, N.Y.: Cornell University.
Cochran, Thomas.
    1968   *The Great Depression and World War II: 1929–1945.* Glenview, Ill.: Scott, Foresman.
Coleman, James S.
    1973   "Loss of Power." *American Sociological Review,* February, 38:1–17.
Commons, John R.; Phillips, Ulrich B.; Gilmore, Eugene A.; Sumner, Helen L.; and Andrews, John B.
    1958   *Documentary History of American Industrial Society,* Vols. 3–6, 9. New York: Russell & Russell.
Commons, John R. et al.
    1966   *History of Labor in the United States.* New York: A. M. Kelley.
Crenson, Matthew A.
    1971   *The Unpolitics of Air Polution.* Baltimore: Johns Hopkins Press.
Cross, Ira B.
    1935   *A History of the Labor Movement in California.* Berkeley: University of California Press.
Cruse, Harold.
    1967   *The Crisis of the Negro Intellectual.* New York: Morrow.
Curti, Merle Eugene.
    1959   *Peace or War: The American Struggle, 1636–1936.* Boston: J. S. Cunner.
Dahl, Robert.
    1961   *Who Governs?* New Haven: Yale University Press.
    1967   *Pluralist Democracy in the United States: Conflict and Consent.* Chicago: Rand-McNally.
David, Henry.
    1958   *The History of the Haymarket Affair: A Study in the American Social-revolutionary and Labor Movements.* 2d ed. New York: Russell and Russell.
Davis, Winfield J.
    1893   *History of Political Conventions in California, 1849–1892.* Sacramento: California State Library, no. 1.

Dearing, Charles Lee.
    1941   *American Highway Policy.* Washington, D.C.: Brookings In-
            stitution.
Desmond, Humphrey J.
    1905   *The Know-Nothing Party.* Washington, D.C.: New Century
            Press.
Destler, Chester McArthur.
    1946   *American Radicalism, 1865–1901.* New London, Conn.:
            Connecticut College Press.
Dillon, John J.
    1941   *Seven Decades of Milk: A History of New York's Dairy In-
            dustry.* New York: Orange Judd.
Dombrowski, James.
    1936   *The Early Days of Christian Socialism in America.* New
            York: Columbia University Press.
Draper, Hal.
    1967   "The Student Movement of the Thirties." Rita Simon, ed.,
            As We Saw the Thirties. Urbana: University of Illinois Press.
Draper, Theodore.
    1957   *The Roots of American Communism.* New York: Viking
            Press.
Dubofsky, Melvyn.
    1969   *We Shall Be All: A History of the Industrial Workers of the
            World.* Chicago: Quadrangle Books.
Dulles, Foster Rhea.
    1940   *America Learns to Play: A History of Popular Recreation,
            1607–1940.* New York: D. Appleton-Century.
    1949   *Labor in America.* New York: Thomas Y. Crowell.
Dumond, Dwight L.
    1939   *Anti-slavery Origins of the Civil War in the United States.*
            Ann Arbor: University of Michigan Press.
    1961   *Anti-slavery: The Crusade for Freedom in America.* Ann
            Arbor: University of Michigan Press.
Earle, Thomas, compiler.
    1969   *Life, Travels and Opinions of Benjamin Lundy.* New York:
            Arno Press.
Egbert, Donald Drew, and Persons, Stow, eds.
    1952   *Socialism and American Life,* Vol. 1. Princeton: Princeton
            University Press.
Eisinger, Peter K.
    1973   "The Conditions of Protest Behavior in American Cities."
            American Political Science Review, March, 67:11–28.
Epstein Melech.
    1950   *Jewish Labor in the U.S.A.: An Industrial History of the*

    Jewish Labor Movement, 1882–1914. New York: Trade
    Union Sponsoring Committee.

Erdman, Henry E.
    1921   *The Marketing of Whole Milk.* New York: Macmillan.

Ferrell, Robert H.
    1968   *Peace in Their Time: The Origins of the Kellogg-Briand
    Pact.* Hamden, Conn.: Archon Books.

Feuer, Lewis
    1969   *The Conflict of Generations.* New York: Basic Books.

Filler, Louis.
    1960   *The Crusade against Slavery, 1830–1860.* New York:
    Harper Bros.

Fine, Nathan.
    1961   *Labor and Farmer Parties in the United States, 1828–1928.*
    New York: Russell & Russell.

Finnie, Gordon E.
    1969   "The Anti-Slavery Movement in the Upper South before
    1840." *Journal of Southern History.* Vol. 35, August.

Fisher, Clyde Olin.
    1922   *Use of Federal Power in Settlement of Railway Labor Dis-
    putes.* Washington, D.C.: U.S. Printing Office.

Flacks, Richard W.
    1967   "The Liberated Generation: An Exploration of the Roots of
    Student Protest." *Journal of Social Issues,* July, 23:52–75.

Floyd, William, ed.
    1925   *Social Progress; A Handbook of the Liberal Movement.* New
    York: Arbitrator.

Foner, Phillip.
    1965   *History of the Labor Movement in the U.S. Vol. 3: The
    Policies and Practices of the AFL, 1900–1909.* New York:
    International Publishers.

Franklin, John Hope.
    1943   *The Free Negro in North Carolina, 1790–1860.* Chapel Hill:
    University of North Carolina Press.

Franklin, John Hope, and Starr, I.
    1967   *The Negro in Twentieth Century America.* New York: Vin-
    tage Books.

Fromm, Erich.
    1941   *Escape from Freedom.* New York: Rinehart.

Galenson, Walter.
    1960   *The CIO Challenge to the AFL.* Cambridge, Mass.: Harvard
    University Press.

Gamson, William A.
    1968a   *Power and Discontent.* Homewood, Ill.: Dorsey.

1968b "Stable Unrepresentation in American Society." *American Behavioral Scientist,* November/December, 12:15–21.

Gamson, Zelda F.; Goodman, Jeffery; and Gurin, Gerald.
1967   "Radicals, Moderates, and Bystanders during a University Protest." Paper presented at American Sociological Association meetings, San Francisco, August.

Garfinkel, Herbert.
1969   *When Negroes March.* New York: Atheneum.

Gitlow, Benjamin.
1940   *I Confess: The Truth about American Communism.* New York: E. P. Dutton.

Goldberg, Joseph P.
1958   *The Maritime Story: A Study in Labor-Management Relations.* Cambridge, Mass.: Harvard University Press.

Gorter, Wytze, and Hildebrand, George H.
1952   *The Pacific Coast Maritime Shipping Industry, 1930–1948.* Berkeley: University of California Press.

Gregory, Paul M.
1956   *The Baseball Player: An Economic Study.* Washington, D.C.: Public Affairs Press.

Hagel, Otto, and Goldblatt, Louis.
1963   *Men and Machines.* San Francisco: International Longshoreman's and Warehousemen's Union.

Harris, Joseph P.
1930   *The Practical Workings of Proportional Representation in the United States and Canada.* New York: National Municipal League.

Hawgood, John A.
1940   *The Tragedy of German-America.* New York: G. P. Putnam's Sons.

Hawkins, Hugh, ed.
1964   *The Abolitionists: Immediatism and the Question of Means.* Boston: Heath.

Hicks, John Donald.
1961   *The Populist Revolt; A History of the Farmers' Alliance and The People's Party.* Lincoln: University of Nebraska Press.

Higham, John.
1950   "The American Party: 1886–1891." *Pacific Historical Review* 19.
1963   *Strangers in the Land: Patterns of American Nativism, 1860–1925.* New York: Atheneum.

Hillquit, Morris.
1965   *History of Socialism in the United States.* 5th rev. and enl. ed. New York: Russell & Russell.

Hirschman, Albert O.
  1970 *Exit, Voice and Loyalty.* Cambridge, Mass.: Harvard Univer-
       sity Press.
Hoag, Clarence G., and Hallett, George H., Jr.
  1926 *Proportional Representation.* New York: Macmillan.
Hoffer, Eric.
  1951 *The True Believer.* New York: Harper & Row.
Hoke, Henry.
  1946 *It's a Secret.* New York: Reynal & Hitchcock.
Hopkins, Charles Howard.
  1942 *The Rise of the Social Gospel in American Protestantism,
       1865–1915.* New Haven: Yale University Press.
Horowitz, Morris Aaron.
  1962 *The Structure and Government of the Carpenters' Union.*
       New York: Wiley.
Howland, Harold.
  1921 *Theodore Roosevelt and His Times.* New Haven: Yale Uni-
       versity Press.
Hughes, Langston.
  1962 *Fight for Freedom: The Story of the NAACP.* New York:
       Norton.
Johnson, Claudius O.
  1967 *Borah of Idaho.* Seattle: University of Washington Press.
Joyner, Fred Bunyan.
  1939 *David Ames Wells: Champion of Free Trade.* Cedar Rapids,
       Iowa: Torch Press.
Kaplowitz, Stan.
  1973 "An Experimental Test of a Rationalistic Theory of De-
       terence." *Journal of Conflict Resolution,* Sept., 17:535–72.
Kaufman, Jacob A.
  1954 *Collective Bargaining in the Railroad Industry.* New York:
       King's Crown Press.
Kellogg, Charles Flint.
  1967 *NAACP, A History of the National Association for the Ad-
       vancement of Colored People, Vol. 1: 1909–1920.* Baltimore:
       Johns Hopkins Press.
Keniston, Kenneth.
  1968 *Young Radicals.* New York: Harcourt, Brace, & World.
Kennedy, David M.
  1970 *Birth Control in America.* New Haven: Yale University
       Press.
Kerner Commission.
  1968 *National Advisory Commission on Civil Disorders: Final
       Report.* New York: Bantam.

Kipnis, Ira.
  1968   *The American Socialist Movement, 1887–1912.* New York:
          Greenwood Press.
Kornhauser, William.
  1959   *The Politics of Mass Society.* New York: Free Press.
Kraditor, Aileen S.
  1969   *Means and Ends in American Abolitionism.* New York:
          Pantheon Books.
Lavine, Harold.
  1939   *Fifth Column in America.* New York: Doubleday, Doran.
LeBon, Gustave.
  1896   *The Crowd.* London: Ernest Benn.
Leiserson, William M.
  1924   *Adjusting Immigrant and Industry.* New York: Harper Bros.
Lenin, V. I.
  1929   *What Is To Be Done?* New York: International Publishers.
Lewis, Orlando F.
  1922   *The Development of American Prisons and Prison Customs,
          1776–1845.* Albany: Prison Association of New York.
Lewis, Walter David.
  1965   *From Newgate to Dannemora: The Rise of the Penitentiary
          in New York, 1796–1848.* Ithaca, N.Y.: Cornell University
          Press.
Lingley, Charles Ramsdell.
  1920   *Since the Civil War.* New York: Century.
Lipsky, Michael.
  1968   "Protest as a Political Resource." *American Political Science
          Review,* December, 62:1144–58.
  1970   *Protest in City Politics.* Chicago: Rand-McNally.
Livernash, E. Robert.
  1961   *Collective Bargaining in the Basic Steel Industry.* Washing-
          ton, D.C.: U.S. Department of Labor.
Lloyd, C.
  1912   *Henry Demarest Lloyd, 1847–1903.* New York: G. P. Put-
          nam's sons.
Lorwin, Lewis.
  1933   *The American Federation of Labor.* Washington, D.C.:
          Brookings Institution.
Lowi, Theodore J.
  1971   *The Politics of Disorder.* New York: Basic Books.
Lutz, Alma.
  1968   *Crusade for Freedom — Women of the Antislavery Move-
          ment.* Boston: Beacon Press.

Lyons, Eugene.
   1941   *The Red Decade: The Stalinist Penetration of America.* Indi-
          anapolis: Bobbs-Merrill.
MacFarland, Charles S.
   1946   *Pioneers for Peace through Religion,* based on the records of
          the Church Peace Union (founded by Andrew Carnegie)
          1914–1945. New York: Fleming H. Revell.
Maddox, Robert J.
   1970   *William E. Borah and American Foreign Policy.* Baton
          Rouge: Louisiana State University Press.
Martin, James Joseph.
   1953   *Men against the State; The Expositors of Individualist Anar-
          chism in America, 1827–1908.* DeKalb, Ill.: Adrian Allen
          Associates.
Marx, Gary T.
   1972   "Thoughts on a Neglected Category of Social Movement Par-
          ticipant: The Agent Provocateur and Informant." Paper de-
          livered at the American Sociological Association meetings,
          New Orleans.
Mason, P. P.
   n.d.   "The League of American Wheelman and the Good Roads
          Movement." Ph.D. dissertation.
May, H. F.
   1949   *Protestant Churches and Industrial America.* New York:
          Harper Bros.
McDonald, David J.
   1969   *Union Man.* New York: Dutton.
McEvoy, James III.
   1971   *Radicals or Conservatives: The Contemporary American
          Right.* Chicago: Rand-McNally.
McKelvey, Blake.
   1936   *American Prisons: A Study in American Social History Prior
          to 1915.* Chicago: University of Chicago Press.
McKenna, Marian C.
   1961   *Borah.* Ann Arbor: University of Michigan Press.
McLaughlin, Martin Michael.
   1948   *Political Processes in American National Student Organiza-
          tions.* South Bend: University of Notre Dame Press.
McNeill, George E., ed.
   1892   *The Labor Movement: The Problem of Today.* New York:
          M. W. Hazen.
McPherson, James M.
   1964   *The Struggle for Equality: Abolitionists and the Negro in the*

Civil War and Reconstruction. Princeton: Princeton University Press.

Metzger, Walter P.
1961 *Academic Freedom in the Age of the University*. New York: Columbia University Press.

Michels, Robert.
1949 *Political Parties*. Glencoe, Ill.: Free Press.

Middleton, Phillip Harvey.
1941 *Railways and Organized Labor*. Chicago: Railway Business Assn.

Mills, C. Wright.
1956 *The Power Elite*. New York: Oxford University Press.

Morris, Richard B.
1970 *Encyclopedia of American History*. New York: Harper & Row.

Morrison, Charles Clayton.
1927 *The Outlawry of War, A Constructive Policy for World Peace*. Chicago: Willett, Clark & Colby.

Muse, Benjamin.
1968 *The American Negro Revolution: From Nonviolence to Black Power, 1963–1967*. Bloomington: Indiana University Press.

Mushkat, Jerome.
1971 *Tammany: The Evolution of a Political Machine, 1789–1865*. Syracuse, N.Y.: Syracuse University Press.

Myrdal, Gunnar.
1944 *An American Dilemma; The Negro Problem and Modern Democracy*. New York: Harper Bros.

Nall, J. O.
1939 *Tobacco Night Riders of Kentucky and Tennessee, 1905–1909*. Louisville, Ky.: Standard Press.

Nevins, Allan.
1935 *Abram S. Hewitt: With Some Account of Peter Cooper*. New York: Harper & Bros.

Nye, Russel B.
1955 *William Lloyd Garrison and the Humanitarian Reformers*. Boston: Little Brown.
1964 *Fettered Freedom; Civil Liberties and the Slavery Controversy, 1830–1860*. East Lansing, Michigan: Michigan State University Press.

Oberholtzer, Ellis Paxson.
1936 *A History of the United States since the Civil War*. New York: Macmillan.

Oberschall, Anthony.
　　1973　*Social Conflict and Social Movements.* Englewood Cliffs,
　　　　　N.J.: Prentice-Hall.
O'Connor, Richard.
　　1968　*The German-Americans.* Boston: Little Brown.
Olson, Mancur, Jr.
　　1965　*The Logic of Collective Action.* Cambridge, Mass.: Harvard
　　　　　University Press.
Paige, Jeffery M.
　　1971　"Political Orientation and Riot Participation." *American So-
　　　　　ciological Review,* October, 36:810--20.
Parsons, Lucy Eldine.
　　1889　*Life of Albert R. Parsons, With Brief History of the Labor
　　　　　Movement in America.* Chicago: L. E. Parsons.
Parsons, Talcott.
　　1960　"The Distribution of Power in American Society." T. Par-
　　　　　sons (ed.), *Structure and Process in Modern Societies.* New
　　　　　York: Free Press.
Payne, George Henry.
　　1912　*The Birth of the New Party.* Atlanta: J. L. Nichols.
Perlman, Mark.
　　1961　*The Machinists: A New Study of American Trade Unionism.*
　　　　　Cambridge, Mass.: Harvard University Press.
　　1962　*Democracy in the International Association of Machinists.*
　　　　　New York: Wiley.
Peterson, Lorin W.
　　1961　*The Day of the Mugwump.* New York: Random House.
Pilisuk, Marc, and Hayden, Thomas.
　　1965　"Is There a Military Industrial Complex which Prevents
　　　　　Peace?" *Journal of Social Issues,* July, 21:67–117.
Pinchot, Amos.
　　1958　*History of the Progressive Party, 1912–1916.* New York:
　　　　　New York University Press.
Polsby, Nelson W.
　　1960　"Toward an Explanation of McCarthyism." *Political Studies,*
　　　　　October, 8:250–71.
Porter, Kirk H., and Johnston, Donald Bruce, compilers.
　　1970　*National Party Platforms, 1840–1968.* Urbana: University of
　　　　　Illinois Press.
Porter, Luther H.
　　1892　*Wheels and Wheeling.* Boston: Wheelman.
Poulshock, S. Walter.
　　1965　*The Two Parties and the Tariff in the 1880's.* Syracuse, N.Y.:
　　　　　Syracuse University Press.

Purcell, Theodore V.
  1953   *The Worker Speaks His Mind on Company and Union.*
          Cambridge, Mass.: Harvard University Press.
  1960   *Blue Collar Man: Patterns of Dual Allegiance in Industry.*
          Cambridge, Mass.: Harvard University Press.
Quin, Mike.
  1949   *The Big Strike.* Olema, Calif.: Olema Publishing.
Quint, Howard H.
  1964   *The Forging of American Socialism: Origins of the Modern
          Movement.* Indianapolis: Bobbs-Merrill.
Rayback, Joseph G.
  1966   *A History of American Labor.* New York: Free Press.
Renshaw, Patrick.
  1967   *The Wobblies: The Story of Syndicalism in the U.S.* New
          York: Doubleday.
Richards, Leonard L.
  1970   *Gentlemen of Property and Standing: Anti-abolition Mobs in
          Jacksonian America.* New York: Oxford University Press.
Ring, Elizabeth.
  1933   *The Progressive Movement of 1912 and the Third Party
          Movement of 1924 in Maine.* Orono: University of Maine
          Press.
Robbins, Edwin Clyde.
  1914   *Railway Conductors: A Study in Organized Labor.* New
          York: Columbia University Press.
Robinson, Jesse S.
  1917   "The Amalgamated Association of Iron, Steel, and Tin
          Workers." Ph.D. dissertation.
Rochester, Anna.
  1943   *The Populist Movement in the United States.* New York: In-
          ternational Publishers.
Rogge, O. John.
  1961   *The Official German Report.* New York: Thomas Yoseloff.
Rogin, Michael Paul.
  1967   *The Intellectuals and McCarthy: The Radical Specter.* Cam-
          bridge, Mass.: M.I.T. Press.
Rogoff, Abraham M.
  1945   "Formative Years of the Jewish Labour Movement in the
          U.S. (1890–1900)." Ph.D. dissertation, Columbia University.
Rollins, Richard.
  1941   *I Find Treason.* New York: William Morrow.
Roney, Frank.
  1941   *Irish Rebel and California Labor Leader: An Autobiography.*
          Berkeley: University of California Press.

Rothman, David J.
  1971 *The Discovery of the Asylum: Social Order in the New Republic*. Boston: Little Brown.
Rowan, Richard W.
  1939 *Secret Agents against America*. New York: Doubleday, Doran.
Russell, Maud.
  1966 *Men along the Shore*. New York: Brussel and Brussel.
Saxton, Alexander Plaisted.
  1971 *The Indispensable Enemy: Labor and the Anti-Chinese Movement in California*. Berkeley: University of California Press.
Schattschneider, E. E.
  1960 *The Semi-Sovereign People*. New York: Holt, Rinehart & Winston.
Schmidt, Emerson Peter.
  1937 *Industrial Relations in Urban Transportation*. Minneapolis: University of Minnesota Press.
Scisco, Louis Dow.
  1901 *Political Nativism in New York State*. New York: Columbia University Press.
Selznick, Philip.
  1960 *The Organizational Weapon*. Glencoe, Ill.: Free Press.
Seymour, Harold.
  1960 *Baseball, Vol. 1: The Early Years*. New York: Oxford University Press.
Smelser, Neil J.
  1963 *Theory of Collective Behavior*. New York: Free Press.
Smith, Robert Miller.
  1961 *Baseball in America*. New York: Holt, Rinehart & Winston.
Sorin, Gerald.
  1972 *Abolitionism: A New Perspective*. New York: Praeger.
Sowles, Patrick.
  1965 "The North Carolina Manumission Society, 1816–1834." *North Carolina Historical Review* 42, January.
Spalding, Albert Goodwill.
  1911 *America's National Game*. New York: American Sports Publishing.
Stampp, Kenneth.
  1943 "The Fate of the Southern Anti-slavery Movement." *Journal of Negro History* 28, January.
Stanton, Elizabeth Cady; Anthony, Susan B.; and Gage, Matilda Joslyn.
  1887 *History of Woman Suffrage, Vol. 1: 1848–1861*. Rochester, N.Y.: Elizabeth Cady Stanton, Susan B. Anthony, and Matilda Joslyn Gage.

Stanwood, Edward.
    1903   *American Tariff Controversies in the Nineteenth Century,
            Vol. II.* Boston: Houghton Mifflin.
Steeger, Henry.
    1969   *You Can Remake America.* Garden City, N.Y.: Doubleday.
Stegner, Wallace.
    1949   "The Radio Priest and His Flock." Isabell Leighton (ed.),
            The Aspirin Age, 1919–1941. New York: Simon & Schuster.
Stein, Leon, and Taft, Philip, eds.
    1969   *Religion, Reform, and Revolution; Labor Panaceas in the
            Nineteenth Century.* New York: Arno.
Stewart, Ethelbert.
    1913   "Two Forgotten Decades in the History of Labor Organiza-
            tions: 1820–1840." *American Federationist* 20.
Stewart, Frank M.
    1950   *A Half-century of Municipal Reform: The History of the Na-
            tional Municipal League.* Berkeley: University of California
            Press.
Stokes, Arson Phelps.
    1950   *Church and State in the United States, Vol. 1.* New York:
            Harper Bros.
Stone, Roy.
    1894   *New Roads and Road Laws in the United States.* New York:
            D. Van Nostrand.
Stoner, John E.
    1942   *S. O. Levinson and the Pact of Paris.* Chicago: University of
            Chicago Press.
Stowell, Charles Jacob.
    1918   "The Journeymen Tailors' Union of America." Ph.D. disser-
            tation, University of Illinois.
Swanberg, W. A.
    1963   *Citizen Hearst: A Biography of William Randolph Hearst.*
            New York: Bantam Books.
Sweeney, Vincent D.
    1956   *The United Steelworkers of America: Twenty Years Later,
            1936–1956.* n.p.
Taft, Philip.
    1964   *Organized Labor in American History.* New York: Harper &
            Row.
Taussig, F. W.
    1888   *The Tariff History of the United States.* New York: G. P.
            Putnam's Sons.
Tcherikower, Elias, ed.
    1961   *The Early Jewish Labor Movement in the United States.* Tr.

and rev. by Aaron Antonovsky. New York: Yivo Institute for Jewish Research.

Thomas, Benjamin P.

1950 *Theodore Weld: Crusader for Freedom.* New Brunswick: Rutgers University Press.

Tilly, Charles.

1970 "From Mobilization to Political Conflict." Center for Research on Social Organization. Ann Arbor: University of Michigan.

1973a "Collective Action and Conflict in Large-Scale Social Change: Research Plans, 1974–78." Center for Research on Social Organization. Ann Arbor: University of Michigan, October.

1973b "The Chaos of the Living City." Herbert Hirsch and David C. Perry (eds.) *Violence as Politics.* New York: Harper and Row, 1973.

1974 "Revolutions and Collective Violence." in Fred I. Greenstein and Nelson W. Polsby, *Handbook of Political Science,* Vol. 3.

Tull, Charles J.

1965 *Father Coughlin and the New Deal.* Syracuse, N.Y.: Syracuse University Press.

Uhl, Alexander.

1954 *Trains and the Men Who Run Them.* Washington, D.C.: Public Affairs Institute.

Vinson, John Chalmers.

1957 *William E. Borah and the Outlawry of War.* Athens, Ga.: University of Georgia Press.

Voigt, David Quentin.

1966 *American Baseball.* Norman, Okla.: University of Oklahoma Press.

Vreeland, Francis McLennon.

1929 "The Process of Reform with Especial Reference to Reform Groups in the Field of Population." Ph.D. dissertation, University of Michigan.

Wagstaff, H. M., ed.

1934 *Minutes of the N. C. Manumission Society, 1816–1834.* Chapel Hill: University of North Carolina Press.

Waite, Frederick Clayton.

1943 *Western Reserve University: The Hudson Era.* Cleveland: Western Reserve University Press.

Warren, Roland L., ed.

1969 *Politics and Ghettos.* New York: Atherton Press.

Wechsler, James A.

1935 *Revolt on the Campus.* New York: Covici, Friede.

Weeks, Stephen B.
    1896   *Southern Quakers and Slavery: A Study in Institutional History.* Baltimore: Johns Hopkins Press.
Wehberg, Hans.
    1931   *The Outlawry of War.* Tr. by Edwin H. Zeydel. Washington, D.C.: Carnegie Endowment for International Peace.
Winkler, Fred A.
    1948   *Railroad Conductor.* Spokane: Pacific Book.
Wohlforth, Tim.
    1960   *Revolt on the Campus: The Student Movement in the 1930's.* New York: Young Socialist Forum.
Wooden, Evans.
    1892   "Labor Troubles between 1834 and 1837." *Yale Review,* May.
Yellen, Samuel.
    1936   *American Labor Struggles.* New York: Harcourt, Brace.
Zald, Mayer N., and Ash, Roberta.
    1966   "Social Movement Organizations: Growth, Decay and Change." *Social Forces,* March, 44:327–41.

Index

211

March on Washington Committee, 20, 83, 151
Marx, Gary, 103
Marx, Karl, 97
Marxism, 4, 44, 57, 100
Mass media, 166–67
Mass society theory, 130–32
Membership, 50
Memorial Day Massacre, 23
Messianic groups, 17
Michels, Robert, 89
Military-industrial complex, x, 10
Mills, C. Wright, 10
Missouri Farmer, x
Mitchell, W. Lindsay, 76
Mobilization, 11, 14–17, 68–71, 82, 89, 112, 137
Modigliani, Andre, ix
Mott, Lucretia, 77–78
Multiple-issue groups, 44–46
Murphy, Charles F., 83
Murray, Philip, 120
Mussolini, Benito, 133

N
NAACP (National Association for the Advancement of Colored People), 83
Nall, J. O., 76
National Female Anti-Slavery Society; *see* Female Anti-Slavery Society, National
National Science Foundation, x
National Socialism, 19
National Student League, 20, 35, 45, 78, 148
National War Labor Board, 119–20
Native American Party, 20, 76–77, 148
Nativism, 20, 43–44, 76–77, 83–84
Negotiation, 32, 140
Negro Labor Congress, American, 158
New advantages, 29, 34–36
New Deal, 118
New entries, index of, 23–24
New look at social protest, 136–41
Night Riders; *see* Tobacco Night Riders
Nixon, Richard, 142
North Carolina Manumission Society, 35, 110, 153

O
Oberschall, Anthony, 136–37
Oehler, 100–101
Olson, Mancur, 55–71
Order of Secularists, 157
Organization, 89–108
Outlawry of War, American Committee for, 16, 20, 64, 146

Outside pressure, 118–22, 140

P
Packinghouse Workers Organizing Committee, 20, 118, 150
Pact of Paris; *see* Kellogg-Briand Pact
Paige, Jeffery, 134
Palmer, Mitchell, 39
Panic of 1873, 77
Pattern maintenance, 90–91
Peace and Freedom Party, 138
Peace research, x
Permeability, x, 1–12, 22, 73, 141–43
Persuasion, 57–58, 68
Philadelphia Journeymen House Painters Association, 158
Philanthropic groups, *see* Universalistic groups
Pilisuk, Marc, x, 10–11
Pinchot, Amos, 42–43
Pittsburgh, Pa., 65
Planter's Protective Association, 53, 69, 75, 82; *see also* Tobacco Night Riders
Pluralism, 5–12, 73, 130–43
Pluralist democracy; *see* Pluralism
Pluralist theory; *see* Pluralism
Police, 2–3, 77, 103, 142, 164–65
Political parties, 8
Political system; *see* American political system
Polsby, Nelson, 135
Poverty, 44
Power, concentration of, 10–11
Power centralization, 92–99, 124–25, 127
  and bureaucracy, 93–96
  defined operationally, 93
  and factionalism, 104
  and length of challenge, 121–22
  and success, 93–96, 107–8
Power elite, 10–11
Power Elite, The, 10
Powerlessness, x
Preemption, 29–30, 35, 51–53, 93, 116, 123
Princeton, Kentucky, raid, 75
Prison Discipline Society, 39
Privileged groups, 63–66, 70
Procedural consensus, 6–7
Progressive Labor Party, 20, 152
Progressive Party; *see* Bull Moose Party
Prohibition, 34, 38
Proportional Representation League, American, 20, 48, 149
Protocols, 25
Public goods; *see* Collective good
Public interest; *see* Collective good
Public opinion, 33

This book has been set in 11 and 10 point Times Roman, leaded 2 points. Chapter titles are 24 point Optima and chapter numbers are 18 point Optima italic. The size of the type page is 27 x 46 picas.